PABLO FANQUE AND THE VICTORIAN CIRCUS

*Further details of Poppyland Publishing titles can be found at*
**www.poppyland.co.uk**
*where clicking on the 'Support and Resources' button*
*will lead to pages specially compiled to support this book*

*Join us for more Norfolk and Suffolk stories and background at*
**www.facebook.com/poppylandpublishing**
*and follow* **@poppylandpub**

with best wishes for a fulfilling retirement.

29 June 2017

# Pablo Fanque and the Victorian Circus

## A Romance of Real Life

by

Gareth H.H. Davies

POPPYLAND
PUBLISHING

Copyright © 2017 Gareth H.H.Davies
First published 2017 by Poppyland Publishing, Cromer, NR27 9AN
www.poppyland.co.uk
ISBN 978 1 909796 32 4
Designed and typeset in 12 on 14.4 pt Gilgamesh
Printed by Lightning Source

Picture credits:

Author 3, 62
Author's Collection 31, 40, 44, 85, 97, 108, 119
Billy Rose Theatre Division, New York Public Library 37
British Library C194.b.305-307 45
Harry Ransom Center, University of Texas 65, 86
Houghton Library, Harvard University 49
*Illustrated London News* Cover, 51, 66, 96
NLIS Picture Norfolk Clare, 25
Poppyland Collection 122
*Punch* 105
Stockport Local Heritage Library 88
World's Fair Ltd. 13

Also by Gareth H.H. Davies

*The Fall of Yarmouth Suspension Bridge: A Norfolk Disaster*
*The Clown King: Popular Entertainment 1840-1860*

# CONTENTS

# Visit to Pablo's

A VISIT to Pablo's during the Fair,
Was a sight, we are sure, surprisingly rare.
Miss Hope, in a manner astonishing, true,
Received from all present the praise which was due.
The Elliotts, for feats, which astonish'd us all,
On a globe danced amazing, with never a fall.
The Youth and the Maiden, in Irish costume,
Gave the trio of Graces an excellent room.
O'Donnell the part of old Pickwick well grac'd,
And passed through his changes with wond'rous haste.
Miss Brown, as if ordinary feats to displace,
Made her Ariel leaps with marvellous grace;
And Williams, nine horses did hold in a rein,
As fast and as steady as though bound in a chain.
Young Hernandez gave pleasure, inspiring to view;
How such feats he can do, we can give you no clue.
While Pablo showed us the ways of the Sailors,
Our minds were distinctly turn'd to the Tailors;
But in the midst of such splendour, brilliant and fleet,
We could think of none others than those in High street;
And as the swift steed through the Circus did run,
We thought them a figure of LEVY and SON,
Whose Coats and whose Vests, are as varied and rare,
As the talent which Pablo and Company do share.
And as for an Overcoat, we are sure you'll find none
Which surpasses, for beauty, those of LEVY and SON.

Advertisement placed for THE EMPORIUM, HIGH STREET,
owned by Levy and Son
Sheffield Independent — 1 August 1849

# Acknowledgements

Arthur H. Saxon notes, in his excellent biography of Andrew Ducrow, "How difficult it is to trace and reconstruct the careers of these early artists ... They travelled prodigiously. Because they were generally held to be of low status in the hierarchy of entertainers and therefore did not merit the same consideration as their brethren in the dramatic profession, their activities frequently went unchronicled in local journals." Saxon's statement is undoubtedly true, when researching the early career of those that would become well known and this historian's task was also hampered by having to meticulously find references in a myriad of local newspapers. This is not necessarily the case today. Searchable online resources enable what previously took years to be done in months. For this I am particularly indebted to the British Newspaper Archive. This resource, which has made much of the British Library's local newspaper collection available online, makes the search for 'where and when', and to some extent 'how' much more accessible.

I am also beholden to museums, libraries and online archive deposits, from Leeds to Texas and Tasmania, for their help in not only making primary sources available, but also responding when queries arose. Finally, I'm appreciative of the Internet Archive (archive.org) and the Google Books Library Project for digitising so much public domain material found in major research libraries and making it available.

Not all research can or should be done on the internet and I'm grateful to the staff at the National Fairground and Circus Archive (University of Sheffield Library) which houses The John Turner Collection. Here can be found the research notes and database of Dr. John Turner, which enables quick searches of performers and provides citations of primary sources that were used in his research. A devotee of the history of the circus, his articles are the only previously written pieces on Pablo Fanque.

Finally, a special thank you must go to Janet, my wife, who acted as a careful and insightful reader for this book, and to Peter Stibbons, at Poppyland Publishing, for taking on the work. Your friendship and encouragement have been invaluable.

Gareth H.H. Davies, 2017

# Introduction

*The Time is approaching when History will be attempted on quite other principles; when the Court, the Senate and the Battlefield, receding more and more into the background, the Temple, the Workshop and the Social Hearth will advance more and more into the foreground, and History will not content itself with shaping the answer to the question: How were men taxed and kept quiet then? But will seek to answer this other infinitely wider and higher question: how and what were men then? Not our Government only, or the "house wherein our life was led", but the Life itself we led there, will be inquired into.*

Thomas Carlyle[1]

In a society in which ethnic diversity and cultural identity is much valued, the exploration of those previously regarded on the fringes of British history is both topical and popular. Examples of successful individuals from ethnic backgrounds have been increasingly sought in the last few decades to enrich our understanding of the past.

Pablo Fanque, or William Darby, the first black circus proprietor, is the perfect illustration of this phenomenon. In modern times his connection with the Beatles song, *Being For the Benefit of Mr Kite*, found on the Sergeant Pepper album,[2] provides a very real nostalgic link for a generation which began to cast off their parents' assumptions about race, class, and notions of history. By the time the album was released, in 1967, the shift towards 'history from below' was already taking hold in academia, stimulated by E.P. Thompson's *Making of the English Working Class* (1963), which aimed to make a connection between an emerging class-consciousness and the popular culture developing in early industrial society. By the time I was reading history at university in the late 1970s, not only was 19th century 'labour history' a strong, and almost unavoidable, course within most history degrees, but Thompson's book was essential reading. Historians following Thompson characterised the patterns of popular culture during the industrial age as 'reconstructing the voices of the poor'. As Professor Rohan McWilliam has stated:

> Given that the personal was political, it followed that it was possible to recover a political project in folk song, sport or the 'rough culture' of the common people. Social historians described how, during the nineteenth century, the carnivalesque dimensions of popular culture were subject to increasing social control by Evangelicalism, the new police force, the middle class and by the capitalist social order with its emphasis on time discipline; all energies had to be harnessed towards the labour process. Respectability was the watchword of Victorian Britain, leaving little room for the often disorderly world of popular recreations. … Popular culture was no longer made by the people but was manufactured for them by the new culture industries. Football, for example, was driven off the streets by the police force and effectively taken away from the working class. It was then remade by the public school system, provided with rules and returned to the people in a commercialised form, played in stadiums for mass enjoyment. The participatory popular culture that existed up to about 1850 had given way to a culture of spectatorship.[3]

Circus, as an aspect of popular culture, was always about the spectator, or spectacular, rather than any subversion from any participatory activity. Its appeal lay in the presentation of the 'unusual' and 'heroic' (in itself an aspect of social control). Indeed 'what the public could not do', rather than presenting the highly developed skills of a recreation in a professional manner. The circus was the ultimate form of spectator entertainment. It professionalised, commercialised and industrialised types of performance that had existed for hundreds of years. The entertainments associated with circus artistes, such as rope-walking, tumbling and acrobatics had a long tradition of drawing audiences at country and town fairs. However, horsemanship, above all, was the essence of the original circus. This had been tightly defined by the form and character of warfare that proclaimed its last gasp at Balaclava in

1854. As the battlefield became increasingly industrialised, the skills of the cavalryman became obsolete, and it was in the circus ring that his expertise found expression. The earliest circus proprietor was Philip Astley, an ex-military man, who used the skills taught him in the army to provide spectacular exhibitions of horsemanship.

There was also a strand of itinerant fairground families providing entertainment at annual fairs who, steeped in horsemanship, would provide horse-breaking services when visiting a community. These became the circus dynasties, such as the Cookes, who relied heavily on generations of family members to perpetuate and grow their business[4]. But there were also the 'jossers'[5], essentially working-class artistes outside these cliques that believed they could do just as well, managing, and possibly owning, their own troupes and establishments. William Darby (Pablo Fanque) was one of these. It was these minor entrepreneurs with deep social roots in the working population that enabled the circus to become properly embedded in popular culture. Some, such as Andrew Ducrow and William Batty, achieved success through innovation and risk-taking. Most failed financially as the commercialisation of this new entertainment industry boomed, becoming the preserve of those with no experience in the ring, but with greater business acumen and deeper pockets.

In the 21$^{st}$ century, Pablo Fanque has become an icon of African British history being the 'Keystone of the Heritage Corner' in Leeds, where his grave can be found. The website asks us to "Discover … the life, times and circus world of Pablo Fanque — and other African-Victorian personalities. These narratives intertwine with the pop-culture revolution of the 1960's — highlighting migration, positive cultural exchange and the rich legacies of diversity today"[6]. If we are to try and understand 'how and what were men then', we must recognise that, as E.H. Carr put it, the historian cannot "divorce himself from the outlook and interests of his age". The fact that William Darby was African British had an important bearing on his life and tells us something about Victorian society, but so does the fact that he was born of very humble origins and became one of the best known and loved circus proprietors of the Victorian period.

This book attempts to investigate the life of Pablo Fanque and shed light on the phenomenon that was the early Victorian circus and its role in popular culture. In doing so it hopes to highlight relevant themes of interest to the student of the period.

1   Carlyle, T. (1838-9) *Boswell's Life of Johnson* in Critical and Miscellaneous Essays Vol. III p. 83.

2   John Lennon stated that the lyrics were inspired by a Rochdale playbill, dated 14 February 1843, for Pablo Fanque's Circus, that he bought in an antique shop.

3   McWilliam, R. *Review of The Beginnings of a Commercial Sporting Culture in Britain, 1793—1850* (review no. 438) — http://www.history.ac.uk/reviews/review/438 accessed 8 March 2016.

4   See McMillian, S. (2012) *Cooke's: Britain's Greatest Circus Dynasty.*

5   Josser — a 20th century circus word for an outsider who performs in the circus but was not born into a circus family — "the boundary between the josser, and the legitimate — that is born and bred — circus person, is permanent. You can't step over that divide and claim the place that blood ties would have granted." Stroud, N. (2000) *The Secret Life of a Circus Girl* p.10.

6   http://heritagecornerleeds.wix.com/heritage-corner accessed 26 February 2016.

# 1

# A Fine City

*Of all the cities I have seen*
*(And few their numbers have not been)*
*This Norwich is the oddest; whether*
*View'd in its parts, or altogether.*

Anon[1].

The history of William Darby's early life in Norwich is obscure. At his death, his date of birth was ambiguous[2]. Eventually it was established he "was born in Norwich on 28 February 1796, the third son of John Darby, a butler of African descent, and his wife, Mary, *née* Stamps"[3], and it is this date that was carved on his gravestone. It is understandable that this date remained unchallenged in biographical writings[4] on William Darby until modern times, given a birth certificate[5] was produced by his manager, Mr. Montague[6],

*Believed to be a photograph of Pablo Fanque circa 1860.*

to establish the fact[7]. However, investigation of the sources suggests that the boy, who later styled himself Pablo Fanque, was actually their fifth child and was born on 30 March 1810[8]. John and Mary's third son, William, who was born in 1796, died on 30 April 1797.

One can speculate why Darby chose to retain a copy of the birth certificate of his older sibling. It might have been an attempt to portray himself older than he was, but, more likely, in an age where reputation mattered, it might have been to disguise the fact he had been born in St. Andrew's workhouse, a pauper child. An alternative and more mundane explanation might be that Montague obtained a copy of the wrong birth certificate.

What we can be sure of is that John Darby and Mary Stamp were married in St. Stephen's, Norwich on 29 March 1791[9]. John, probably of African origin, had been born in November 1766 in St. Augustine's parish, being named after his father. Mary Stamp was born in Great Ryburgh, Norfolk in September 1768. While John could only leave his mark on the marriage register, she was literate enough to sign her name. It is impossible to say whether Mary was also of African origin or when John's paternal line arrived in Britain, but the records suggest that William was at least second generation African British.

Establishing the ethnic origin of individuals from documents and other sources during this period is difficult. Names were almost entirely anglicised, however there is evidence of other African British individuals living and working in Norwich during this period. For example, two 1823 paintings among a set of 52 by John Dempsey, an itinerant illustrator of miniatures, show a bootmaker named 'Black Charley' and 'Cotton', a haberdashery street seller.

The presence of Africans in Great Britain went back to Roman times, but in the 17th and 18th century there was an increase in black settlement, particularly in London. Black slaves were attendants to sea captains and ex-colonial officials, as well as to traders, plantation owners and military personnel. This created an increasing black presence in the northern, eastern, and southern areas of the capital. There were also black seamen from West Africa and South Asia. Slavery was never legal in England, and the Cartwright decision of 1569[10] had determined that any man or woman brought to England effectively gained their freedom. This status was cemented by a variety of 18th century court cases[11]. Africans living in cities such as Norwich were most likely to be freed slaves themselves or the offspring of slaves.

The campaign to end slavery in the British colonies had gathered momentum during the last half of the century, culminating in the Abolition of the Slave Trade Act in March 1807. Norwich, and the wider county of Norfolk, with its libertarian culture, was active in the cause of abolition. One central figure was William Stevenson, the owner of the Norfolk Chronicle newspaper, which assiduously reported anti-slavery activity throughout the country. Stevenson was a member of the Society of United Friars[12], a philosophical Norwich society that also did charitable works, including the annual distribution of bread and soup to the poor of the city. Members made it known that they would only vote for 'Representatives of the People' that also supported abolition[13].

Political pressure for abolition was a natural consequence of Norwich's radical traditions. There were a significant number of Norwich citizens that supported the ideas of Thomas Paine[14], leading to the city being referred to in common gossip as "that city of sedition"[15]. This radicalism dating back to Tudor times, but at the turn of the 19th century this was characterised by a number of factors. Economic prosperity, powered by the textile industry, meant one of the widest franchises in the country. The ability to vote was governed by admission to the Freedom of Norwich. In theory, in order to trade one should be a freeman, but, since this right included financial obligations, in many provincial cities it was ignored. Norwich was built on the weaving industry and the prosperity of journeymen weavers since Medieval times meant there was a high proportion of freemen. When times got tougher in the 19th century, they were not afraid to use their collective political muscle.

Norwich also had an important minority of religious dissenters. The Presbyterians included a large body of well-to-do citizens. In 1756 they had built the Octagon, which John Wesley described in the following year as "the most elegant in Europe"[16]. The Independents had built a baroque meeting house close by, which came to be known as the Old Meeting. The Baptists had their meeting house in St. Mary's. The Quakers not only had a meeting house in Goat Lane, but had also built a substantial building in the Gildencroft, Over-the-Water. While the Methodists maintained the Tabernacle.

This mix of liberal principles and non-conformity from Norwich's 'middle class' created a culture of tolerance and philanthropy to those that were obviously different. Nevertheless, the working people of the city, who protected their industry and work fiercely, mistrusted outsiders as much as anyone in the Kingdom. This is characterised by the word used for Dutch Flemish and Walloon refugees, known as 'Strangers', in the late 16th century.

If one is to gain insight into what it was to be of African descent in Norwich during this period, there is no better illustration than the account of Ukawsaw Gronniosaw[17].

Gronniosaw was an African prince sold into slavery, who for a time lived and worked in Norwich. His short autobiography was narrated to W. Shirley and published in 1810. Having been sold to Mr. Vanhorn, a resident of New York, where his purpose was to "wait at table and tea, and clean knives", he was then sold to Mr. Freelandhouse, who, on his death, freed him. He eventually made his way to Britain. In his account he states how he was treated in Norwich:

> I had at this time an offer made me of going to Norwich, and having constant employ. My wife seemed pleased with this proposal, as she supposed she might get work there in the weaving manufactory, being the business she was brought up to, and more likely to succeed there than in any other place; and we thought as we had an opportunity of moving to a town where we might both be employed, it was most advisable to do so; and that probably we might settle there for our lives. ... When she came to Norwich, I hired a room ready furnished. I experienced a great deal of difference in the carriage of my master from what I had been accustomed to from some of my other masters; he was very irregular in his payments to me: My wife hired a loom, and wove all the leisure time she had, and we began to do very well, till we were overtaken by fresh misfortunes. Our three poor children fell ill of the small-pox, this was a great trial to us, but still I was persuaded in myself we should not be forsaken. I did all in my power to keep my dear partner's spirits from sinking; as her whole attention was now taken up with the children, she could mind nothing else, and all I could get was but little to support a family in such a situation, besides paying for the hire of our room, which I was obliged to omit doing for several weeks; but the woman to whom we were indebted would not excuse us, though I promised she should have the first money we could get after my children came about, but she would not be satisfied, and had the cruelty to threaten us, that if we did not pay her immediately, she would turn us all into the street.

The apprehension of this, plunged me into the deepest distress, considering the situation of my poor babes if they had been in health, I should have been less sensible of this misfortune. But my God is still faithful to his promise, raised me a friend: Mr. Henry Gurdney, a quaker, a gracious gentleman, heard of our distress, and sent a servant of his own to the woman we hired our room of, paid our rent, and bought all the goods, with my wife's loom, and gave it us all. Some other gentlemen hearing of his design, were pleased to assist him in these generous acts, for which we never can be thankful enough, after this, my children soon came about, and we began to do pretty well again; my dear wife worked hard and constant when she could get work, but it was upon a disagreeable footing, her employ was so uncertain, sometimes she could get nothing to do, and at other times when the weavers of Norwich had orders from London, they were so excessively hurried, that the people they employed were obliged to work on the Sabbath-day, but this my wife would never do, and it was a matter of uneasiness to us that we could not get our living in a regular manner, though we were both diligent, industrious, and willing to work. I was far from being happy in my master, he did not use me well, I could scarcely ever get my money from him; but I continued patient, till it pleased God to alter my situation.

My worthy friend Mr. Gurdney, advised me to follow the employment of chopping chaff, and bought me an instrument for that purpose. There were but few people in the town that made this their business besides myself, so that I did very well indeed, and became quite easy and happy. But we did not continue long in this comfortable state, many of the inferior people were envious and ill-natured, and set up the same employ and worked under price on purpose to get my business from me, and they succeeded so well that I could hardly get any thing to do, and became again unfortunate: Nor did this misfortune come alone; for just at this time we lost one of our little girls who died of a fever: This circumstance occasioned us new troubles, for the baptist minister refused to bury her because we were not their members; the parson of the parish denied because she had never been baptized: I applied to the quakers, but met with no success; this was one of the greatest trials I had ever met with, as we did not know what to do with our poor babe: At length I resolved to dig a grave in the garden behind the house, and bury her there; when the parson of the parish sent to tell me he would bury the child, but did not choose to read the burial service over her. I told him I did not care whether he would or no, as the child could not hear it.

We met with a great deal of ill treatment after this, and found it very difficult to live: We could scarcely get work to do, and were obliged to pawn our clothes, we were ready to sink under our troubles; when I proposed to my wife to go to Kidderminster, and try if we could do there.

The Darby family must have experienced similar hardship to Gronniosaw. The onset of the French war brought considerable problems for the working poor of Norwich[18]. The price of bread fluctuated, but generally tended in the upwards direction, and those seeking help from the parish increased. In order to relieve this pressure, the Court of Guardians purchased wheat and sold it on at a reduced rate to bakers in the city to try and stabilise the weight of a loaf[19]. Certainly within a year of their third child's death, in 1797, the family found themselves in St. Andrew's workhouse, where Mary gave birth to a girl, Mary Elizabeth, on 18 March 1798. The fact that this child died in the workhouse three years later and that William was born there in 1810 may be an indication that the family never escaped destitution for any significant period of time.

The St. Andrew's workhouse was one of two maintained by the 32 parishes within the city and its outlying hamlets. Situated in Bridge Street, it was part of the remains of the Black Friary. It was greatly enlarged in 1802 to provide accommodation for about 600 inmates. The able-bodied were employed in the manufacture of worsted and cotton goods. A separate infirmary was located in the parish of St Clement, just beyond St Augustine's Gate, in what was formerly a Lazar house founded by a bishop of Norwich. It accommodated up to 130 infirm and paupers aged 65 or over. The other Norwich workhouse was situated in the run-down former palace of the Duke of Norfolk, in the parish of St. John's.

Frederick Eden, in his report on the state of the poor in 1797 describes St. Andrew's:

The Poor are maintained principally in two large Workhouses, one formerly a palace of the Duke of Norfolk, and the other a monastery. It is not surprising, therefore, that they should be in many respects extremely unfit for the purpose to which they are now applied. The latter, more especially, is dark and confined, and from the great number of paupers in it (about 700) exhibits rather an uncleanly appearance. There are about 40 beds, (generally of straw,) in each chamber. The room, where the victuals are served out, has two doors; through one of which, the Poor enter, one by one, to receive their allowance; go out by the other door; and carry their victuals up to their bed-rooms, where they are allowed to dine, sup, &c. The Poor in the house are chiefly women and children: they are employed in schools, under the superintendence of task-masters, in spinning worsted.[20]

William Darby's early life was therefore shaped by the severe economic depression of the period. Although the war ended in 1815, the economic depression continued. In January 1817 a meeting of the inhabitants of the city was called by the Mayor to discuss the relief of the poor. The *Norfolk Chronicle* reported that one Alderman stated that, "the grand purpose was to find Employment, but he was not prepared to state how that could be done … perhaps the Paving of part of the city might suggest itself to their minds; this would employ many bricklayers and other labourers now destitute of work, if the material were to be had; as far as gravel at Thorpe, he would give it *gratis* for this purpose. Nearly 3000 applications for out-door relief have been made to the Court of Guardians, and there were nearly 700 poor persons in the Workhouse: it was truly painful to see honest laborious men applying for relief and more painful still for not having the means of giving them employment."[21]

Later sources tell us that William Darby was apprenticed to William Batty, the equestrian and circus proprietor. The Poor Relief Act of 1601 allowed the parish officials to bind a child to a master. Originally children could be apprenticed from the age of seven, but in the early 19th century the age was raised to ten. The child was originally bound until the age of 24, but this was lowered to 21 in 1778.[22] One might expect William's apprenticeship to have taken place between 1820 and 1831, but there is no record of William Darby being apprenticed from St Andrew's workhouse during this period[23]. Those apprenticeships ordered by the Guardians in the minute books are all to 'respectable' trades such as chimney sweeps or weavers in the city[24], and no doubt a request to become an itinerant circus performer would have been rejected[25]. It is most likely that William's apprenticeship occurred when his family was not in the workhouse and by personal arrangement. It was common practice in the nineteenth century that many children came into the circus profession by other means[26].

How William Darby became apprenticed to William Batty we may never know. The plight of the poor in Norwich during the French wars may have made the city fertile ground for circus proprietors to recruit and train children. Indeed, William Darby was not the first person born in Norwich to enter the profession and form his own equestrian troupe:

> The Equestrian and Pantomime Company, now exhibiting at Harper's Pantheon[27], by far excels every thing of the kind that has been witnessed here for some time past. The surprising sagacity of Sydney's Dogs, and the pantomimical talents of Mrs. Usher, and that of the infant child, are exceedingly interesting. It is somewhat surprising that Mr. Clarke[28] should make so great a progress in the equestrian art in so short a period; he is a native of Norwich, and it is well known that he has not been in the profession more than four years. The comic abilities of Mr. Usher[29], as Clown, keep the audience in continued roar of laughter. — A new Ballet of Action is announced for this evening.[30]

The attraction of an itinerant life as a vaulter or leaping over horses must have been compelling. For the working poor, not only were these artistes admired for their physical skills, but also for the fact that they had somehow escaped into a different world. Although ticket prices to these performances were often beyond the pay of a working man, showmen visiting the city were only too keen to make allowances to enable the working poor to visit their shows. In January 1819, George Wombwell, whose menagerie became one of the most popular at fairs throughout the country and would in the future appear alongside Pablo's circus, stated in one advertisement, " … as G.W. wishes to gratify the curiosity of all ranks, he will admit poor labouring hands as low as 6d. each."[31]

Advertising was also key to maintaining audiences for the period they were in a city or town. One example of a more outlandish promotion was the challenge thrown down to Clarke by Dimond, 'The Flying Huzzar', who was appearing with Adams[32] equestrian troupe, in December 1818:

---

# PANTHEON
## RANELAGH GARDENS, NORWICH

---

A Challenge to Mr. Clark for 100 Guineas, offered by Mr. Dimond.

SOME short description of the above Wager is most respectfully offered to the public by DIMOND, the Flying Huzzar. — It is now three weeks since he had the honour of appearing before the public at the Pantheon, and feels ambitiously thankful for the very flattering manner he has been received.

On a late occasion the Pantheon, was visited by Clark. (the Mountebank) who pursued me in a private matter to make himself acquainted with the apparatus Dimond leaps by.

On the 28th of Dec. last he published similar fetes [sic] of leaping to be performed by him at Diss — and in the bills of that day he was pleased to use Dimond's name, as also the Flying Huzzar. — Without wishing to distract any merit Clarke may possess, I hereby offer him the above Wager of 100 Guineas (or any sum he can conveniently meet) to leap over a fixed object, to be performed before the public at the Pantheon any evening Clark may choose to appoint during the performance here. Mr. Dimond is ready to appoint an umpire any moment Mr. Clark will give him a meeting upon the subject.

**An Answer is expected.**

Clarke was to reply robustly in the Chronicle of 19 January:

### An Answer from Mr. Clarke to Mr. Dimond's Challenge for 100l.
### Mr. DIMOND

SIR — If I were to pass unnoticed the challenge you have sent me through the medium of this paper, I should reflect much on myself. Your appellation I laugh at, as coming from one, whose head is as shallow as the object he kicks at most evenings.

If you think the method you have adopted, thus publicly to challenge me without cause or reason will raise you in public favour, you are mistaken, as they will find that not only is your challenge you advance gross falsehoods, but in the very bills that are printed for the Pantheon.

If you are the Flying Hussar don't fly from the truth.

You accuse me of pursuing means in a private manner, to make myself acquainted you hop by. How is that possible, when you advertise that you have no apparatus whatever attending your performances. Again, my visit at the Pantheon; it was so private, that I paid my admission-money, gave my ticket, and mixed among those that were in the Circus. Oh! Mr. Dimond fide you are made the tool of those that will repeat the word Mountebank, as appertaining to one of your family, I mean J......s D........d.

If I quoted your name in the bills of the 28th of Dec. at Diss, I thought that instead of depreciating your merit, I was adding to your fame as I condescended to say (in the same manner as Mr. Dimond the Flying Hussar.)

Now, Sir, I not only accept your challenge for 100l, but five if you think fit, to go through the various Feats of Leaping I advertised in my bill of the 28th of Dec. But let it be impressed on your mind, and that of Messrs Adams your managers upon when I might retaliate as Mountebanks, but I will say late Quack Doctors, Punch and Judy Exhibitors from the West of England, that if a trial of skill take place between us, another place must be appointed instead of the Pantheon as this far fetched challenge is made to answer many purposes, not only for Mr. F.......h's[33] bung and spicket, but for the late Quacks to pocket the receipt of that evening, laugh at the public, you, and myself. Let the Prussia Gardens[34] or any other public place be named in the vicinity of Norwich.

I am not fond of a paper war, and will answer nothing else but what is immediately to the purpose.

I remain yours

**J. CLARKE, Equestrian**

P.S. Your idea and that of your Managers was not bad, in hopes of having a full house for once in a way, but it proves abortive.

Diss, Jan 14th, 1819.

Mr. Dimond failed to respond but Clarke made the most of the publicity when he appeared at the Tombland Fair in April:

---

### TOMBLAND FAIR
**J. CLARKE,**
*EQUESTRIAN,*

BEGS to announce, to the Nobility, Gentry, and inhabitants of Norwich and its vicinity, that he proposes erecting a RIDING SCHOOL at the above Fair, on Thursday, April 8, 1819, on the Castle Ditches. J.C.'s numerous Company and admired Stud Horses will attend, added to which, and independent of Miss Clarke's unrivalled exertions on the Tight Rope; &c. he will through his flying Art of Horsemanship, with Oranges, Forks, &c which defies any horseman in England to surpass, and that the public may be satisfied that it was not without pretensions that he accepted Mr. Dimond's Challenge, he will go through the whole of the Leaps introduced at the Pantheon, viz. the Garter through the Hoops, over a number of Horses, Sec. &c. &c. For particulars see the handbills of the day.[35]

---

In looking for evidence as to how William Darby became a circus performer, it is clear that artistes regularly visited the popular city fairs, or were attractions at the many taverns and smaller pleasure gardens within Norwich and its environs. Travelling 'circuses', although they were not necessarily described as such, came at particular times of the year. These took place either at the Pantheon or occasionally on the Castle Meadow. One of the first established circuses to visit during this period was Thomas Cooke's in 1820.

Thomas, the founder of Cooke's circus dynasty, was an accomplished rider, acrobat and ropewalker. In November 1806 he fitted up a former iron foundry on the Southside of the Seagate in Dundee and called it 'Cooke's Olympic Circus'. The next year he opened his 'New Olympic Circus' in Virginia Street, Aberdeen. In December 1820, his Olympic Circus was at the Pantheon, Norwich in which:

> T. Cooke will introduce his GRAND TRAMPOLINE, where
> he will THROW SOMERSETS THROUGH SMALL HOOPS,
> Three feet in diameter — likewise OVER a NUMBER of
> HORSES; and lastly will THROW HIS WONDERFUL
> SOMERSET THROUGH SIX BALLOONS.[36]
> Mr. Finch was to invite the Cooke family back to Ranelegh
> Gardens the following year for his benefit in which they:
> Most respectfully beg leave to announce to the Nobility,
> Gentry and others of Norwich and its Environs, they have
> engaged the PANTHEON with a SELECT COMPANY of
> EQUESTRIANS,
> *ROPE DANCERS &c.*
> FROM
> Astley's Royal Amphitheatre
> *With Part of That;*
> BEAUTIFUL STUD OF HORSES
> FROM THE
> *Theatre Royal, Covent Garden*[37]

A number of secondary sources repeat the fact that William Darby appeared for the first time in Norwich on 26 December 1821, as 'Young Darby', with William Batty's company[38], but this fact is contentious. Cooke's circus was the only recognised circus in Norwich during this period, and no mention is made of a 'Young Darby' performing. Dr. Turner's extensive notes on Fanque, held at the National Fairground and Circus Archive,[39] do not mention such an appearance.

Indeed, the first recorded appearance of Batty's circus in the city did not occur until 2 March 1840 and this included Pablo Fanque in the entourage[40]. There were however earlier connections between Batty and Norwich. In October 1828, The Hull Packet records that Batty's Olympic Circus attended their town fair and included a "number of extremely clever hands (from the Royal Pantheon, Norwich)"[41]. There was also a connection between Batty and Richard Bullard, the Norwich brewer. He certainly invested money both in Batty's enterprises and in Pablo Fanque's circus and was later to claim he had known William Darby "from infancy"[42].

*The interior of Victoria station, Norwich, showing the rotunda. The former circus building is being incorporated into the station. This was an official photo of the Great Eastern Railway.*

Whatever, the truth of William Darby's origins he, as one newspaper put it, "was trained in a good though severe school, that of the late Mr. Batty, of Astley's Circus and he never forgot the rough and practical lessons he there received"[43].

1   Anon. (1792) *A Norfolk Tale* ... p.32. cited in Cornfield P.J. *From Second City to Regional Capital* — Rawcliffe, C. and Wilson, R (2004) Chapter 6, *Norwich Since 1550*.

2   Many newspapers reported that he had been born in 1804, and was therefore 67 years of age. However, the *Leeds Times*, 13 May 1871 p.5. in noting his age was 75 remarked, "To any one who was not acquainted with his age, the impression would have been produced that he was only about fifty years old, so active was he in the saddle, so full of anecdote in conversation with his acquaintance, and so quick in arranging the details of his business."

3   Turner, J.M. 'Fanque, Pablo (1796–1871)', *Oxford Dictionary of National Biography*, *Oxford University Press*, 2004; online edn, Jan 2009 — http://www.oxforddnb.com/view/article/53827, accessed 7 March 2016 — Turner takes John Darby's occupation from the marriage certificate of William to his second wife, Elizabeth in 1848.

4   To date, the most significant work on Pablo Fanque was done by Dr. John Turner, who is best known as the author of the *Dictionaries of British Circus Biographies*. See https://www.sheffield.ac.uk/nfa/collections/turner accessed 23 March 2016.

5   Civil registration of birth did not take place until 1837, so an original 'birth certificate' could not have been produced by Montague. However, when civil registration began the Registrar General printed forms to enable certified copies of a parish register entry to be supplied to members of the public for legal purposes such as proving rights under probate. Montague, or William Darby must therefore have obtained what was correctly called 'a certified copy of an entry in a register'.

6   W. H. Montague was a circus manager, who was at one time employed by many of the main English circus proprietors, including Pablo Fanque.

7   *The Era* — 14 May 1871 p.4. — "As some doubt has been expressed respecting Mr. Pablo's age, the following copy of the certificate of his birth, with which we have been favoured by Mr. Montague, may be interesting to our readers:-'William, son of John Darby and Mary, his wife, late Mary Stamps, spinster, was born in Norwich, Norfolk February 28th, 1796; privately baptised February 28th 1796, as it appears by the Register Book of All Saints' Parish. Ed. Press, Assisting Minister.'"

8   *England, Norfolk Poor Law Union Records, 1796-1900*, images, FamilySearch — https://familysearch.org/pal:/MM9.3.1/TH-267-12395-232381-86?cc=1824706 — accessed 15 March 2016, Norfolk > Norwich > St Andrew's Workhouse > Baptisms > image 29 of 83; Record Office, Norwich.

9   *England Marriages, 1538–1973*, database, FamilySearch — https://familysearch.org/ark:/61903/1:1:NXNT-XXK, accessed 15 March 2016 — John Darby and Mary Stamp, 27 Mar 1791; citing St. Stephen's, Norwich, Norfolk, England, reference Item 10 p 61; FHL microfilm 1,471,611.

10  In 1569, Cartwright was observed savagely beating another, which in law would have seen as battery, unless he could mount a defence. Cartwright stated that the man was a slave whom he had brought to England, and thus such punishment was not unlawful, but the court held that the man must be freed.

11  *Shanley v Harvey* (1763) - the Lord Chancellor held that as soon as a person set foot on English soil he or she became free, and that a 'negro' might maintain an action against his or her master for ill usage, together with an application for habeas

corpus if detained. *Somerset v Stewart* (1771-72) - A writ of habeas corpus had been issued to secure the release of James Somersett, a negro confined in irons on board a ship arrived in the Thames from Virginia, bound for Jamaica, and the return stated that he was a slave under the law of Virginia. The court ordered 'the black must be discharged' and that a slave could not be made to leave England against his will. This case was widely understood as freeing slaves in England.

12  Thomas Ransome, a clerk at Gurney's bank, founded the United Friars in 1785. The society ambition was to emulate the intellectual endeavours and love of learning and philanthropy of monastic orders. Each member was assigned to an order of monks or friars and were required to wear the appropriate habit and to acquaint himself with the history of his order. The society elected an 'abbot' every year who would act as Chairman and conveyor of meetings.

13  *Norfolk Chronicle* — 18 February 1792 p.3. — "THE Society of UNITED FRIARS, and for the PARTICIPATION USEFUL OF KNOWLEDGE, considering the Abolition of the Slave Trade as an OBJECT of HUMANITY, cannot but express their hope, that the exertions for this purpose may prove successful and they further feel themselves bound, the same SACRED Principle of HUMANITY, to support those Gentlemen ONLY, as proper Representatives of the People, who vote for the annihilation that most INIQUITOUS TRAFFIC in human flesh. Feb. 7, 1792. W. WILKINS, Abbot."

14  Born in Thetford, Paine was among the first revolutionists to call for a declaration of American independence from the British monarchy and his writings were decisive in the eventual decision of the Continental Congress to issue its Declaration of Independence on 4 July 1776. Paine had returned from America in 1787 and, in the 1790s, he began to immerse himself in political affairs, this time in support of the French Revolution. In 1791-2, Paine published his most important contribution to political philosophy, the Rights of Man, in which he defended political rights for all persons on the grounds of their natural equality under God and concluded that only a republic founded on the democratic principles could protect the equal rights of all citizens.

15  Brightwell, C.L. (1854) *Memorials of the Life of Amelia Opie* p.43. — https://archive.org/details/memlifeameliaoooopierich accessed 23 March 2016.

16  *Wesley's Journal*, vol III, p.325.

17  His anglicised name being James Albert.

18  Eden, F. M. (1797) — *The State of the Poor or an History of the Labouring Classes in England* p.487. — "the expenses for the Poor of this city, have, in general, of late, considerably increased. This, it is probable, may be attributed to the War, and other causes, which have occasioned a great stagnation of trade in Norwich."

19  *Ibid.* 13 — 8 August 1795 p.2. — "The Court of Guardians, with an attention to the necessities and distress of the poor highly commendable, have lately purchase several hundred sacks of flour, which is now selling to the bakers of this city at a reduced price, in order to enable them to bake at the present assize, which must unavoidably have been lessened at least one-sixth, had not the Court taken this judicious step."

20  *Ibid.* 13 — p.479.

21  *Ibid.* 13 – 4 January 1817 p.2.

22  See more at: http://www.genguide.co.uk/source/apprenticeship-indentures-parish-poor-law/42/#sthash.i7nbT6fg.dpuf, accessed 8 March 2016.

23  *Guardians of Poor Court minute books 1813-1833*, Norfolk Record Office (NCR Case 20e/I-15, available on microfilm MF/X/356-357) – apprenticeships recorded in the minutes list children from the age of 10 to 14 and for periods up to seven years.

24  Eg. entry of 4 April 1820 – "Ordered that Jacob Horth of Saint Clement aged 11 be bound apprentice to William Wharf of Saint John Maddermarket Chimney Sweeper until 16 years of age to be allowed 40 /- with the usual Cloathing [sic]"

25  One example of this is the case of Mary Stevens, a 13 year old apprentice of Pablo, who ran away. Pablo took out a summons against her for absconding in March 1858. In court the magistrate agreed with the defence that 'horse dancing or horsemanship' was not a 'trade or handicraft' and therefore dismissed the action. *Wells Journal* – 20 March 1858.

26  One example concerning Fanque appeared in the Norfolk News in its 'News in Brief' section of 11 January 1851. The paper reported that a strolling beggar in Cork had sold his son for 2 shillings, aged 14, to Pablo Fanque to be 'trained in equestrian feats'. This story, repeated in other regional newspapers at the time, was however, refuted in the Cork press – "We understand there was no truth in the statement which appeared in our last paper with respect to the alleged sale of a boy to Monsieur Pablo Fanque. The lad was regularly indentured, and his father, so far from receiving a sum of money, was very glad that his son should be afforded so good an opportunity of earning a profitable livelihood. Monsieur Fanque, we are sure, from his character, would be incapable of taking part in any unworthy transaction." – *Cork Examiner* – 3 January 1851 p.2.

27  The Pantheon was a large octagonal building about seventy feet in diameter, with space for an orchestra and capable of accommodating about twelve hundred people. It was surrounded by a garden lit by gas lamps (originally called Ranelagh but renamed the Victoria Gardens), which contained a bowling green, bars and other facilities. Today this area is occupied by Victoria House near St. Stephen's roundabout. The Gardens closed in 1850, when the land was acquired by the Eastern Union Railway for use as their terminus, and many of the buildings sold for demolition. Part of the Pantheon was utilised as the new station – see http://www.heritagecity.org/research-centre/at-leisure-in-norwich/the-circus-in-nineteenth-century-norwich.htm accessed 8 March 2016.

28  Clarke had performed first at the Pantheon in the autumn of 1813, both as an equestrian and within the 'Troop of Flying Phenomena, consisting of surprising Leaps, and Summersets' – *Ibid.* 12 – 9 October 1813 p.3.

29  Dicky Usher was one of the most celebrated clowns of the ring, and known for his stunts and wagers to draw crowds for his benefit night. He is the first recorded clown to 'sail in a washtub drawn by geese' in July 1818, but also was known to drive a chariot pulled by cats.

30  *Ibid.* 13 – 30 September 1815 p.2.

31  *Ibid.* 13 – 9 January 1819 p.2.

32  The brothers Adams had visited The Pantheon regularly since 1817 with their

troupe. Their equestrian feats were supplemented by tight and slack rope walking and other circus type acts. In 1818, they employed performers to add a pantomime and burletta to their show, for which a stage was erected in the Pantheon.

33 Finch, the owner of the gardens at this time. The Ranelegh Gardens were sometimes known as Finch's Gardens.

34 The Prussia Gardens was one of the smaller pleasure gardens associated with the King of Prussia tavern on the Ipswich Road. Like Ranelegh Gardens, it hosted entertainments such as balloon ascents and fairground feats. For example, in 1815, a Mr. Steward attempted a balloon ascent. The 50,000 crowd that gathered, having paid their money, tore the balloon to pieces when it failed to ascend. The car, or basket, was mounted by a chimney sweep and paraded around the city in triumph. Mr. Steward, who was badly injured, was only saved from the mob by General Money, who took him to a place of safety. See *Ibid.* 12 – 11 February 1815 p.2.

35 *Ibid.* 13 – 3 April 1819 p.3.

36 *Ibid.* 13 – 2 December 1820 p.3.

37 *Ibid.* 13 – 8 December 1821 p.3.

38 Eg. Hobbs, C. *The Hendersons Were Not There (neither was Mr Kite) - Sheffield 1848* – http://www.chrishobbs.com/sheffield/hendersons.htm accessed 15 March 2016.

39 *John Turner Collection NFA 0063, box files 9 –13.*

40 *Ibid.* 13 – 29 February 1840 p.2. – "BATTY's ROYAL CIRCUS, CASTLE MEADOW, NORWICH, WILL OPEN ON MONDAY 2nd MARCH 1840 ... Mr. BATTY, Proprietor of the Royal Amphitheatres, Dublin and Manchester, in claiming the honour to address the Nobility, Gentry, and others of the city and county of Norwich and Norfolk, begs to state that after many years labour and research in this country and on the Continent, he has succeeded in procuring an entire stud of diminutive PALFRIES, with WILD ZEBRAS, and some the most beautiful LEOPARD HORSES ever yet witnessed in this part of England. His Company too embraces the most eminent Performers in every Department of his hazardous Profession, in it will be found Mons Plege, from Franconis, Paris, the greatest Tight Rope Dancer in the world, (and who will perform the opening night), the Brothers Messrs. J. & W. Daly, Messrs. Leonard, Wilkinson, Charlton, Ludovic, Fanque, Lee, Walker, Newsome, Fuller, Polaski. &c. &c. Mr. Batty will have the honour of appearing twice first night."

41 *Hull Packet,* 14 October 1828 p.2 & 3. – "OLYMPIC CIRCUS, MONS. BATTY respectfully announces to the Inhabitants of Hull, that he has Opened a large commodious CIRCUS, in Mr. KIRKWOOD's YARD, opposite Wellington-Street, where a great variety of EQUESTRIAN and other PERFORMANCES will be exhibited by the celebrated Company from the Royal Pantheon, Norwich."

42 See Chapter 5.

43 *Ibid.* 7 – 13 May 1871 p.5.

2

# The Flying Spirit of the Storm

*The cord beneath the dancer springs;*
*Aloft in air he vaulting swings;*
*Anon he whirls the flip flap round,*
*In somersets his limbs rebound;*
*Distorted now, now prone depends,*
*Now with elastic force ascends;*
*The crowd, in wonder and delight,*
*With clapping hands applaud the sight.*

Norfolk Chronicle — 21 March 1840

Although William Darby's roots in circus performance can be difficult to trace, his 'apprenticeship' followed a well-worn path, first being trained as an acrobat, and then in horsemanship[1]. The circus, as a commercial enterprise, had brought together these two distinct forms of entertainment, the older being that of the fair and street performers such as acrobats, tumblers, somersaulters and vaulters. Recruitment into the circus was usually within the family, with children from a very early age being trained by their parents to perform in the act. Children, with the charm of innocence, appealed to an audience that marvelled at the suppleness of the performers and the seeming ease of their exertions and contortions. Henry Mayhew, in his interview with an acrobat, or 'street posturer', gives us an indication of not only how hard the training was, but also how performer 'apprenticeships' often ignored the legal requirements of the day:

My father was a tumbler, and in his days very great, and used to be at the theatres and Richardson's show[2]. ... He brought me regular up to the profession, and when I first came out I wasn't above two years old, and father used to dance me on my hands in Risley's style, but not like Risley[3]. I can just recollect being danced in his hands, but I can't remember much about it, only he used to throw me a somersault with his hand. The first time I ever come out myself was a piece called 'Snowball,' when I was introduced in a snowball; and I had to do the splits and strides. When father first trained me, it hurt my back awfully. He used to take my legs and stretch them, and work them around in their sockets, and put them up straight by my side. That is what they generally call being 'cricked,' and it's in general done before you eat anything

STREET ACROBATS PERFORMING.

*Street acrobats performing from Henry Mayhew's "London Labour and London Poor, Vol III"*

in the morning. O, yes, I can remember being cricked, and it hurt me terrible. He put my breast to his breast, and then pulled my legs up to my head, and knocked 'em against my head and cheeks about a dozen times. It seems like as if your body was broken in two, and all your muscles being pulled like Indian rubber.

I worked for my father till I was twelve years of age, then I was sold for two years to a man of the name of Tagg, another showman, who took me to France. He had to pay father 5l. a year, and keep me respectable. I used to do the same business with him as with father, — splits, and such-like …[4]

Some acrobats had not grown-up with performance in their blood. Another interviewee, Lewis Nelson, (professional name Signor

Nelsonio), became a 'Street Risley' against his parents' wishes. The description of his early career shows how vulnerable children were to being exploited by showmen:

> The reason why I took to the Risley business was this. When I was a boy of seven I went to school, and my father and mother would make me go; but unfortunately, I was stubborn, and would not. I said I wanted to do some work. 'Well,' said they, 'you shan't do any work not yet, till you're thirteen years old, and you shall go to school.' Says I, 'I will do work.' Well, I wouldn't; so I plays the truant. Then I goes to amuse myself, and I goes to Haggerstone-fields in the Hackney-road, and then I see some boys learning to tumble on some dung there. So I soon began to do it too, and I very soon picked up two or three tricks. There was a man who was in the profession as tumbler and acrobat, who came there to practise his feats, and he see me tumbling and says he, 'My lad, will you come along with me, and do the Risley business, and I'll buy you your clothes, and give you a shilling a week besides?' ...
> One day, instead of going to school, I went along with this man into the streets, and then he did the Risley business, throwing me about on his hands and feet. I was about thirteen years old then. ... Then I got chucking about, à la Risley, my little brother, who was about seven years old ...
> Soon after I met my old friend the swallower again, in Ratcliffe highway. I was along with my little brother, and both dressed up in tights and spangled trunks. Says he, 'Oh, you will take to tumbling will you? Well, then, come along with me, and we'll go in the country.' Then he took us down to Norwich (to Yarmouth); then he beat me, and would give me no clothes or money, for he spent it to go and get drunk.[5]

Mayhew's interviews with itinerant entertainers show that most aspired to continuity of work by being employed by circus proprietors, fair booth owners or theatre managers during the pantomime season. To act alone or in small troupes on the streets, at city and town fairs or in the pleasure gardens of small public houses, was seen as a 'drop' and inevitably financially more precarious[6]. Only an elite achieved regular seasonal work with the established proprietors of the day. Some, like the Cookes, had family members to draw on, but most required a turn-around of fresh acts to keep audiences coming back during their stay in a town. The skill of the performer was all-important and new and more daring routines became necessary to retain a reputation.

It was in Leicester, at the end of 1833, where Pablo started building his reputation on the "Corde Fluxo" with Batty's circus[7]. He was to remain with Batty for the troupe's winter tour. At the next port of call, in Brighton, his evolutions on the rope were described as "astonishing, though looked on by the spectators, particularly the ladies, not without trembling"[8], and it was during its stay here that the troupe performed before the Royal family on 3 January 1834. Their next venue was Southampton and the advertisement placed in the Hampshire Advertiser described the troupe as, "… decidedly the largest in the Kingdom; consisting of Forty Male and Female Performers of the first-rate talent, with a stud of Foreign and British Horses, and Six Ponies — the Smallest in Europe; also headed by a superior Military Band"[9]. Pablo was billed as:

> PABLO FANQUE, The American Voltigeur and
> Flying Mercury, will make his first appearance here,
> And exhibit his Performances on the
> CORDE VOLANTE[10],
> Upon which he is not surpassed by any Performer in
> Gymnastic Exercises.[11]

Today one imagines a big-top tent as being the basis of a touring troupe, but early nineteenth century circus proprietors would build a wooden building in situ if performing in a town for several weeks.

Mr. Batty's Circus opened on Monday evening, with a promise of great success. The building is of immense size, affording convenient accommodation to the most crowded audiences. The boxes are tastefully fitted up, and the great extent of the Circus (equal, we should think to Astley's Amphitheatre,) permits the display of numerous equestrians in an act of horsemanship, and enables Batty to give such scenes as the Knights of Palestine, performed this week, with all the effect such an extensive area affords. The band is efficient and well conducted, and the whole building is handsomely illuminated with gas.[12]

The following week Batty described what spectators might expect from Pablo's performance:

> The Entertainments will commence with
> FEATS OF LEAPING,
> By Pablo Fanque, the man of Colour, the loftiest jumper in England, who will take a number of surprising leaps without the assistance of any elastic apparatus — first, over a garter 12ft high — second, through a hoop, 2ft 6in, in diameter — third, through cross hoops — fourth, through a balloon[13] 2ft 9in in diameter — fifth through two balloons — sixth, through a military drum 4ft 6in long — seventh, will take a surprising leap over 10 horses — eighth, will leap through a hoop of real steel daggers — and lastly an unparalleled leap over
> A POST CHAISE, LENGTHWAYS![14]

Such acrobatic and gymnastic feats in the ring were highly dangerous and an artiste took risks with his or her life every performance. Batty's troupe were about to leave for Liverpool and would have been reminded of the profession's dangers when the news of the death of a pole 'percher' at one of the city's theatres reached them.

O'Donnell, a well-known clown had brushed with death in 1830 while performing his balancing act at the top of a pole[15]. He was not so lucky now in 1834:

## CORONERS' INQUESTS

In our last number we gave the melancholy death of a performer at the Queen's Theatre named O'Donnell and on Saturday last an Inquest was held upon the body, when it appeared by the evidence of Mr. Wells, one of the equestrian performers at the Queen's Theatre, that the deceased was standing on his head on a pole in the circle when he met with the fatal accident which caused his death. The pole stood about twelve feet high. There is a small wooden bowl fixed on the top, the diameter of which at the broadest is about four inches. In this bowl O'Donnell placed his head, with his feet directly upright, when performing this feat. He used to stand on his head on the pole from four to five minutes, but he had scarcely been up half the time when the accident occurred as above stated, and he fell from nearly the top of the pole to the ground, a height of eight or nine feet. He lay motionless and speechless on the floor, and assistance was immediately rendered him.

Mr. Bradbury (another witness) said that he had been speaking to him before he went on the pole, and he seemed intoxicated. After he was bled he was carried to a house within two doors of the Theatre, and when Frederick Hilder went to see him he said, "Fred, it is all over with me; be a friend to my wife and children."

The unfortunate man has left three children, the eldest about six years, the youngest about eight months old. He lingered until half-past seven on Thursday morning, and grew delirious about two o'clock. He was rather fond of liquor, but was considered a harmless unoffending man. The Jury returned a verdict of "Accidental Death."[16]

The attraction of the circus was built upon the audiences' admiration for the skill and muscle of horse and human alike. It was defined by the 'real' and 'unhidden' performance of the artistes. These were no 'actors' performing a 'role' but performers depending on their raw 'force' and ability in the ring. Circus performance was about demonstrating the 'impossible'. As Yoram Carmeni has put it, "Circus not only claims to be real; it publicly claims to be the really impossible. In the performers' daily conversations these claims are supposed to show the public 'something they [the public] cannot do'. That which 'they cannot do' is dramatised by invoking primordial experiences, staging phenomena which are in themselves recognized and established metaphors of the extremes of human experience, classical symbols, carrying their own proof. ... When applied to acrobatic routines, the claim for 'that which they cannot do' refers to what is staged as real and obviously difficult as well as unique dexterity necessary for the performance of the various routines. Perhaps most emphatically referred to is the staging of the real and obvious risks taken in the aerial acts — the danger"[17].

Pablo's early career with Batty relied on his youth, physical strength and ability, but although intrinsically dangerous, acrobatic and gymnastic feats were only interludes between the 'main action' which was equestrianism. It is clear that commentators of the period recognised that Batty was bringing additional vibrancy to this art:

*Royal Amphitheatre.* — It happens but too frequently that equestrian performances, however excellent they may be, become, from constant repetition, monotonous and unexciting. This impression has evidently been foreseen by Mr. Batty, who has fully obviated it by judiciously infusing variety into each succeeding entertainment. Last week we had cause to speak in high commendation of the feats of horsemanship and agility. This week we have been equally pleased with the many scenes entirely new to a Liverpool audience, and have justly elicited the unanimous applause of brim-full houses. The death of Shaw, the Life Guardsman[18], by Mr. Hickin; was most effectively portrayed. The exhibition on the flying-rope, by Pablo Fanque; and the postures, scarcely human, by the Polish Brothers were exceedingly clever. The most astonishing performance during the evening was a scene by Mr. Batty; — in it are combined all the beauties of other acts of riding, with the immense difficulty of governing six high-mettled horses at full speed, which in Batty's hands, change their position and pace instantaneously, — at one moment in pairs, then abreast, or in single line, forming a rapid whirl which the eye can scarcely follow. Having seen the great Ducrow, we were not prepared to witness so perfect a display of fearless and intricate equestrianism as Batty exhibits; but in this respect we must avow our conviction of Batty's superiority. Excellent performances of the kind, and cheap prices, continue to draw good houses.[19]

By the time Pablo returned to Norwich with Batty, in the spring of 1840, he was still starting the performance with "his extraordinary leaps and other gymnastic feats", but the programme now included Mr. Mosely, "in proper costume" portraying "the wild Indian of the North American Prairie, coursing round the arena on his fleet horse, and using his bow, spear and canoe paddle, with uncommon dexterity and clever effect. Master Newsome and Miss O'Donnell, in the courtship of Jockey and Jenny afforded a bold display of infant equestrianism, and danced the highland fling with much spirit and comic expression. Mr. Wilkinson's personations of Shakespeare's Falstaff, Shylock and Richard the Third, all executed at full speed on horseback ... A vaulting match afterwards gave the gymnastic members of the company an opportunity of shewing their respective powers, in which Messrs. Wilkinson, Daly and others, as usual, took a prominent part. In these trials the Herculean Lee threw twenty somersets in succession, a wonderful proof of muscular force as well as of athletic skill. Then followed a well-appointed troop of equestrians, as Spanish cavaliers and ladies, making a splendid entrée, on Mr. Batty's numerous stud, under the able direction of Mr. Smith, the riding master of the establishment. Mr. Batty himself at length appeared, in the costume of

THE WILD YOUNG PERUVIAN, by Mr Wilkinson.
at Mr DUCROW'S Amphitheatre.

*The Wild Young Peruvian, by Mr Wilkinson, at Mr Ducrow's amphitheatre.*

a Russian Courier; he distinguished himself equally by adroitness and intrepidity, whilst performing the promised feat of riding and managing a number of his well-trained horses. The crowning gem of the night's performance was the rope-dancing of Mons. Plege. It is one of the finest exhibitions of the kind that we recollect ever to have seen."[20]

It was the equestrians that were the stars of the Victorian circus and Batty provided the role model for the ambitious William Darby. It is clear that, in order to succeed in this emergent and swiftly growing entertainment industry, it was horsemanship that would distinguish you from the rest. While Batty aspired to the fame of Astley or Ducrow, Darby aspired to be Batty and become one of this elite band of equestrians.

1   The training of circus children followed a carefully prescribed route, which is described in the *Town* for 17 October 1840. It began with posturing at around five years of age and progressed to balancing, gymnastics, stilt walking, slack wire, tightrope, dancing, combat with the broadsword, musical instruments and riding in entrées. The pupil eventually arrived at a single act of horsemanship — cited in Saxon, A.H. (1978) *The Life and Art of Andrew Ducrow & The Romantic Age of English Circus.*

2   Richardson's Theatrical Booth was one of the largest fair show booths of the period and said to be 30 metres (100 feet) long and 9 metres (30 feet) wide, with an audience capacity of 1500 people. — Kennedy, D. (2010) *The Oxford Companion to Theatre and Performance* p.197.

3   A Risley or 'Risley business' is where the performer lies on his back and supports one or more children, known as 'flyers', using only his feet. The act is named after Richard Risley Carlisle (professional name, Professor Risley), an American acrobat, who perfected the technique around 1840-1841 with his two daughters.

4   Mayhew, H. (1861) *London Labour and the London Poor Vol. III* p.90.

5   *Ibid.* p.95-96.

6   *Ibid.* p.91. — "I ... began pitching in the street. I didn't much like it being a regular performer, and looked upon it as a drop. ... At Glasgow I got a pound a day. ... The fair is a week. And after that one of our chaps wrote to me that there was a job for me, if I liked to go over to Ireland and join Mr. Batty, who had a circus there. ... I stopped a twelve month with him, and we only did four towns and the troupe did wonders."

7   *Leicester Chronicle* — 30 November 1833 p.2.

8   *Brighton Gazette* — 16 January 1834 p.3.

9   *Hampshire Advertiser* — 15 February 1834 p.1.

10  Corde Volante — an aerial rope that is rigged in a 'v' or 'u' shape. The performer sits in the middle and performs tricks while the rope is swinging.

11  *Ibid.* 8.

12  *Ibid.* 8 — 22 February 1834 p.2.

13  Balloon — a hoop with paper stretched over it that would be broken as the performer went through.

14  *Ibid.* 9 — p.3.

15  *Ibid.* 8 — 25 November 1830 p.3. — "Mr. O'Donnell, the clown at the theatre, fell a few nights ago from a pole twelve feet high, at the top of which he was turning upon his head. Fortunately, although much hurt, he was able to perform the next night."

16  *Morning Post* — 24 March 1834 p.3.

17  Carmeli, Y.S. (1990) *Performing the "Real" and the "Impossible" in The British Traveling Circus* — Semiotica 80—3/4 p.203.

18  John (Jack) Shaw (1789–1815) would have been well known to the audience as a pugnacious boxer and hero of Waterloo. Noted for his very powerful physique and great strength, he was a skilful rider and swordsman. While going to the aid of Captain Edward Kelly of his regiment (2nd Life Guards), Shaw was isolated by French cuirassiers when his sword broke in his hand. Striking fiercely about him with his helmet, he was eventually unhorsed and cut down by his opponents, receiving numerous wounds. Shaw was seen later that night, lying dreadfully injured on a midden near La Haye-Sainte, and in the morning his lifeless body was buried nearby. His body was later exhumed and returned to Britain at the instigation of Sir Walter Scott, who had met him in the studio of the artist Benjamin Haydon, where Shaw posed as a model. A cast of his skull is in the Household Cavalry Museum in Windsor. John Haskins' 1816 poem, *The Battle of Waterloo: A Poem in Two Cantos*, immortalised Shaw as follows:

"Nor 'mongst her humbler sons shall Shaw e'er die,
Immortal deeds defy mortality."
19  *Liverpool Mercury* — 31 October 1834 p.6.
20  *Norfolk Chronicle* — 21 March 1840 p.2.

# 3

# Dreams of Wonder

*Cut the dialect and come to the 'osses.*

attributed to Andrew Ducrow while
watching a rehearsal of Hamlet.

Just behind Marine Parade on the seafront at Great Yarmouth can
be found one of only two of Britain's surviving purpose-built circus
buildings. The Yarmouth Hippodrome was built by the showman
George Gilbert on the site of his original wooden building. By the time it
was constructed in 1903 the heyday of such buildings was long past, but
the name, 'hippodrome' gives away the nature and origins of this form
of amusement, for it was foremost an equestrian activity.

PHILIP ASTLEY.

Born Jan.ʳ 8ᵗʰ 1742

*'Twas here the Painter's Task to trace*
*But the more Semblance of his Face,*
*The Portrait of whose Mind, more true,*
*Lo! his own Work presents to view.*

*Philip Astley in silhouette.*

If one is to appreciate the popularity of
Pablo Fanque, we need to understand the
relationship between entertainment and
the horse from the late 1760s onwards.

In 1768, Philip Astley, a former Sergeant-
Major in the 15th Light Hussars, established
a riding school on a fenced wayside field
on Lambeth Marsh. Calling himself the
'English Hussar', he performed feats such
as straddling two cantering and jumping
horses, doing headstands on a pint pot
on the saddle and a 'parody of riding by
a foppish tailor'. He would charge 6d.
admission or 1s. for a seat. Astley never
referred to his entertainment as a circus, but
called the arena a 'circle' or 'amphitheatre'.

His business soon grew and by 1777 he had a large wooden building by Westminster Bridge.

Astley's Amphitheatre was to define the form and structure of the circus. Its ring diameter of 42 feet, the tightest riding circle at which his horse could gallop without changing gait, was ideal, as centrifugal forces ensured that the rider's feet were pushed against the rump of the horse making it easier to stand and perform acrobatics.

Astley's original business was predominately a riding school and horse-taming establishment, with additional amusing entertainments when exhibitions of riding took place.

> The True and Perfect Seat on Horseback — There is no creature that yields so much profit as the horse; and if he is made obedient to the hand and spur, it is the chief thing that is aimed at. Mr. Astley undertakes to break in the most vicious horse in the kingdom, for the road or field, to stand fire, drums, &c.; and those intended for ladies to canter easy.
>
> His method between the jockey and the ménage, is peculiar to himself; no gentleman need despair of being a complete horseman that follows his directions, having eight years experience in General Elliott's regiment.
>
> For half-a-guinea he makes known his learning (teaching) any horse to lay down at the word of command, and defies any one to equal it for safety and ease.[1]

Astley also began touring with his riding school, arriving for the first time in Norwich in 1776, as testified by his advertisement in the Norfolk Chronicle:

---

**ASTLEY's**

New RIDING-SCHOOL, in Conisford, Norwich,
WILL be open'd on TUESDAY next, being the 8th of October,
with a Variety of manly Feats of Activity.
The brilliant TEMPLE of MINERVA;
Consisting of various capital Pieces of Mechanism, never
exhibited in Norwich, will be Open for Inspection. Also
several pleasing Amusements, taken from the BOULEVARDS
of PARIS; particularly a surprising Exhibition,

---

With uncommon large living SERPENTS,
Many of which live to extend twenty-one Feet, as may be seen
in the Course of this unaccountable Exhibition.— the SLACK
ROPE will be exhibited,
The ROASTED PIG.
Great Variety new FEATS of ACTIVITY on HORSEBACK, Mr.
Astley, Mr. Griffin, Mr. Phillips, Mrs. Griffin, and the Clown.
Mr. Astley will go through the different Exercises of the
Broad Sword — Towards the Conclusion of the Evening's
Entertainment,
LOFTY TUMBLING and VAULTING,
In a Manner truly entertaining. The Lion and Salmon's Leap,
flying over Chairs and Tables, by several capital Performers.
The EGYPTIAN PYRAMIDS;
Or, LA FORCE D'HERCULE.
Will be display'd, with considerable Alterations. In short, the
Entertainments will be exhibited in a most brilliant Stile [sic].
The Doors to be open'd at Four, and to begin at Half past Four
o'Clock precisely. Admittance, Seats 2s, Riding School 1s.[2]

From the very beginning women were also part of the equestrian
performance, and Astley's wife, Petsy, known as "La Fille de l'Air" added
her own particular skill to the show:

ASTLEY's grand curious EXHIBITIONS, from LONDON.
Most assuredly the last Week of exhibiting in the City
Norwich.
At the RIDING-SCHOOL, Conisford;
This present Evening, also on Monday, Tuesday, and Wednesday next,
THE USUAL DIVERSIONS, Mrs. ASTLEY will command a
large HIVE of BEES quit their Habitation and assemble on her
Arm, representing Lady's Muff:
She with uncommon Art, and matchless Skill,
Commands those Insects to obey her Will:
With Bees all cruel Means apply,
To kid the Cow for her Milk, the Hen for the Egg, or the Sheep

She takes the Honey, but them doth not destroy.
for the Fleece it bears, would certainly be an Act of Cruelty: If
a Mode could be laid before the Public, to prevent the annual
Destruction of that useful Insect, such an Object would be
commendable — This Exhibition proves there is a Probability.
The grand TEMPLE of MINERVA,
(Surprising to all) will be open at Three o'Clock, and
exhibiting to the Company until Four o'Clock, at which Time
the Curtain of the Temple to descend, and a general Display of
the several Exhibitions to immediately commence. Admission
— Front Boxes Two Shillings. Side Boxes One Shilling. Back
Places Sixpence.[3]

Exhibitions of horsemanship were of course not necessarily unique[4] and, like tumbling, vaulting and other types of amusements, had been performed at fairs, taverns and other venues in the past. What made Astley distinctive was the type of performance that he drew from his military experience, the establishment of the specific configuration of the venue to display that performance to best effect, and the nature and form of the entertainment that took place within it. With regard to the former, the art of horse-dancing, or ménage, was a particular skill developed for controlling the horse on the battlefield, and had been the preserve of the aristocratic elite, who made up the lighter cavalry in Charles I's Civil War army. This is exemplified in its starkest sense by William Cavendish, Duke of Newcastle, and his "Love … for good horses" during Charles II's reign[5]. Cromwell's New Model Army had ensured that such skills were no longer the preserve of the upper class. By the Seven Years War, in which Astley had fought, ménage was inevitably part of cavalry training, whichever class of recruit you were.

The demonstration of these highly professional and militaristic skills provided a significant allure to those seeking the excitement and adventure of performance. It added the potential for romance and the hero worship of those that could perform in synergy with an animal. It is no wonder that it was the horsemen and women that commanded the greatest admiration and respect from audiences that attended the Victorian circus.

*William Cavendish, Duke of Newcastle.*

Astley and his successors went on to develop spectacular, staged representations of battles and the hippodrama (dramas specifically written to include horses) in which the horses were admired as much as the performers, if not more.

Although Astley's first performances were in the open air, by the 1780s he had not only established his permanent amphitheatre near Westminster bridge, but others in provincial towns. The interior of these amphitheatres was not unlike other theatres of the period with a proscenium stage. Spectators were divided into the pit, boxes and galleries, but the pit was mostly taken up by the ring, enclosed by a barrier about four feet high. Astley's third amphitheatre, built in 1804, had an adjustable proscenium[6] by which the stage could be extended from forty to sixty feet in width. Platforms running the entire width of the stage could be raised and lowered mechanically to add depth to the scenes being performed, and were strong enough to support galloping horses and carriages.

By the early years of the nineteenth century the programme at Astley's followed a standard pattern that was to be adopted by other circus proprietors. The performance began at 6.30, with a featured hippodrama, such as "Timor the Tartar" or "The Blood Red Knight". At 8.30 half-price tickets would become available, and the ring was used to house the additional spectators to view the remaining scenes of the drama. Next came "Scenes from the Circle", in which the ring was cleared and spectators were moved to the stage. These scenes took place in the ring and involved gymnasts, acrobats, clowns and the inevitable displays of horsemanship. This lasted some forty five minutes before the audience returned to the ring and the action reverted to the stage, where a burletta[7], pantomime or melodrama rounded off the evening. It was not unusual for these performances to end after midnight or one o'clock.

By the mid-1850s, there were many 'hippodromes' like Astley's with its ring in the centre of the auditorium and its proscenium stage at one end. Even traditional theatres, like Drury Lane, would be converted to contain a ring for hippodramic performance (in this case on the stage itself). Such was the influence and popularity of this form of entertainment that newly built theatres introduced technology to accommodate the

*Astley's third Amphitheatre, 1808.*

provision of horse and circus performances. One example was the New Standard in Shoreditch:

### THE NEW STANDARD THEATRE

The East-enders have now their Amphitheatre of Cirque Olympique, for equestrian performances, which the proprietors of the New Standard Theatre have just provided for, in a novel and ingenious manner.

This little Temple of Drama was erected a few months since, on the site of twelve houses adjoining 'the Standard Theatre,' by Mr. John Gibson, for the proprietors, Messrs. Johnson and Nelson Lee. It faces the Terminus of the Eastern Counties Railway, in Shoreditch. The interior is of the horseshoe form, and a domed roof, a construction peculiarly well adapted for the transmission of sound. The proscenium is 30 feet wide by 30 feet in height, the auditory has a circle of ten private and fourteen public boxes, which, with the pit and gallery, will accommodate 2200 persons. It is lit by a cut-glass chandelier; the front of the two boxes are coloured in two drabs, relieved with gold mouldings, pilasters, equestrian medallions, &c.

The equestrian performances were the holiday novelty of Monday last; but in the place of the stage; for which purpose the flooring is, by ingenious machinery removed upon a kind of railway, the proscenium boxes are made to recede, and a ring is presented 39 feet in diameter, wherein Mr. Cooke and his Stud first exhibited on Whit Monday.[8]

Throughout the heyday of Victorian circus, it was Astley's Amphitheatre that was regarded as the spiritual and 'ancestral' home of the circus under the management of two of the most admired equestrians of the period, Andrew Ducrow and William Batty.

Ducrow was regarded as the greatest equestrian of the age and took over the lease of Astley's Amphitheatre in February 1825.

Ducrow's performances won him not only the widest recognition among his contemporaries but also the admiration of all that came after him. He was probably the first to use the term 'poses plastiques' to describe a particular style of equestrian performance in the ring:

> MR DUCROW will repeat his last new scene, wherein he represents, upon a single horse, without quitting his saddle, seven different characters called, SEPTEM IN UNO; OR, ONE A COMPANY.[9]

Ducrow would pose in character costume on horseback perfectly motionless, as his steed galloped around the ring. He would then take centre 'ring' to pose in recognisable classical forms, known as 'attitudes':

> Amongst a succession of other striking Equestrians in the Circle, MR DUCROW has invented, for this occasion, three New Scenes. He will appear on his rapid Courser, in a Rustic and Heroic Picture, called
> ANDREW, THE MOUNTAIN SHEPHERD.
> AND
> ROB ROY.
> This attempt, Mr Ducrow is bound to confess as complimentary to the national honour of his Friends and numerous Patrons in Edinburgh.
> The Second New Classical Scene
> Bears the title of
> THE LIVING STATUE;
> OR,
> MODELS OF ANTIQUES.
> Wherein will be represented by Mr. Ducrow on a pedestal in the centre of the circle, the following Portraitures:
> 1—6, HERCULES and the NEMEAN LION in Six Attitudes.
> 7, CINCINNATUS, the Roman, fastening his Sandals.
> 8, HERCULES throwing LYSIMACHUS into the Sea.
> 9, The Slave REMOULEUR (The Grinder).
> 10, The Beautiful Poses of the FIGHTING GLADIATOR.
> 11, The Group of HOMER and ANTIGONA.
> 12, ROMULUS, from David's Picture of the Sabines.
> 13, REMUS'S Defence, from the same.
> This representation will conclude with Three of the positions of the DYING GLADIATOR.[10]

Ducrow would go on to train his horses to 'act' in the tableau:

Who has not heard of the astonishing feats of this the greatest horseman who ever existed or will exist? Their tractability in this respect goes beyond anything that could be disposed. There is one beautiful white horse, in particular, which wins all hearts. Perhaps he is the favourite of the stud. He enters the circle in front of the stage alone, with zephyr like wings attached to his shoulders, given to him the character of Pegasus: he bounds or rather flies round the circle several times, as if in ecstatic consciousness of superiority; his mane and tail erect, his fine eyes glistening, and his open nostrils displaying a brilliant red: so sleek, so elegant is this animal, that he is sufficient to occupy the attention of the spectators for a time. Mr. Ducrow enters during this excitement, with peculiar beauty of effect, as Apollo, habited in white, bearing a small harp, delightingly classical. The sounds from the harp attract the attention of Pegasus; he is, as it were, charmed, and becomes the gentle observer of the wishes of Apollo. After a few caresses, Apollo mounts, and standing on the bare back of the spirited animal commences a series of graceful attitudes, while the harp is occasionally touched in unison with the elegance of the performance. After twenty circuits or more, terminating with surprising fleetness of the horse and dexterity of the rider, Apollo springs on the ground; Pegasus rests himself in the centre of the circle, where a tranquil display of reclining attitudes and of beautiful groupings takes place. — Apollo and Pegasus being white, and seen under a powerful brilliancy, they appear in extraordinary lustre, altogether presenting a classical illustration of Apollo and Pegasus resting on Parnassus. This exhibition offers to the eye of taste a series of beautiful compositions, fraught with associations of a character richly poetical and highly gratifying.[11]

However, his greatest contribution was his characterisation in hippodrama. The Courier of Petersburg was his most famous and enduring piece, in which he did the 'grand écart' or split over the backs of five horses. First performed at Astley's, on 7 May 1827, a bill for the week of 28 May describes the action:

*Ducrow invented the scene "The Courier of St Petersburg" in which he rode and managed as many as nine horses at once.*

The Courier received his Dispatches, and is prepared to proceed on his journey — His Four Horses are in readiness, on their backs are surmounted banners bearing the names of the Four great Countries through which he has to pass, viz. *Russia, Austria, France,* and *England,* but otherwise having no covering nor trappings whatever, whereby to assist the Rider, anxious to depart, they are soon urged forward by the Courier with characteristic zeal, and measure the Ground at their Swiftest Speed; the striking of the Clock distantly heard, announces his near approach to the place of relay, where he refreshes, and starts with renewed vigour. — In the Second and Third Part of the Scene, he shews his mastery in the management of the rein, by impelling his Horses through all the changes & paces of equal and unequal galloping, distancing them in all directions, putting them apart, bringing them up again, placing them in all possible situations, disposing them angularly, diagonally, extending them in a parallel line, circuitously, &c. &c.

— And lastly, by making with the manifest difficulty of such a Feat, HE MAKES A COLOSSAL STRIDE over the Five Backs of his Steeds without breaking their Speed; he reposes on their backs when he becomes fatigued, and finally arrives at his supposed destination within the time his exertions would bespeak him to be limited.[12]

Fanque was first to appear at Astley's in May 1839, where, "In the course of the evening, Pablo Fanque, The Flying Indian, will execute his wonderful exercises on the Slack Rope"[13]. It was some years later, in March 1847, after he had formed his own circus, that Pablo was to return to Astley's. Now the accomplished equestrian, he was to impress the audience with his *haute école*:

## ASTLEY'S

We paid a visit to Astley's on Wednesday evening, to see a most extraordinary display of what may be effected by careful training of the horse. Mr. Pablo Fanque is an *artiste* of colour, and his steed goes through a variety of paces with a regularity and apparent intelligence which we have not only never seen surpassed, but never equalled. In all other trotting and dancing trained horses, whose performance it has been our lot to witness, there has always been a certain degree of difficulty in getting them to the required measure of the time to which they were presumed to be stepping, and after that the band has had to accommodate its time to the action of the horse, throwing the bars of the accompaniment into all sorts of time. With Mr. Fanque's horse we observed nothing of this. The steed — a beautiful animal, by the way, who offered a spirited contrast to the conventional nags of the arena — went into his time and paces at once, and sustained both throughout each division of the performance with very singular regularity. This was more generally observable in his dancing, to one or two well-known ballet-airs in different times; but the intricate and difficult road-paces into which he was put by his clever rider, were no less astonishing or worthy of the highest praise, and drew forth loud applause. The exhibition alone will well repay a visit to Astley's; and we recommend it to the patronage of our readers. ... Mr. Pablo Fanque was *the* hit of the evening.[14]

*Astley's – Pablo Fanque and his Trained Steed. (1847)*

Pablo had decided to set up his own circus with the goodwill of many. William Wallett, in his autobiography[15] states that this occurred at Oxford (July to August 1841)[16], during a tour with Batty's circus. On 8 June, Astley's had burnt to the ground. Batty had immediately left the tour while in Dublin to secure it for himself[17]. On his return he told his company, "Thirty years ago I said I would one day be master of Astley's …". Although Ducrow had attempted to support the Astley family in plans to rebuild, ill health meant that he eventually announced his retirement in favour of William Batty. Ducrow was to die on 27 January 1842.

Andrew Ducrow was a pivotal figure in the history of the circus, coining the word and concept of the 'hippodrama'. As William T. Moncreiff, the famous dramatist of the time, recalled in 1851:

Ducrow was of all masters of the horse the greatest; it was his genius and enterprise that erected the modern circus. He found it, as it has been happily said, a mere ring for ground and lofty tumbling, for buffoonery and rough riding; and he made it a scene of picturesque, rational and chivalric entertainment, full of dramatic and olympian attraction.[18]

His period of management at Astley's, from 1825 to 1841, transformed 'circus' into a mainstream performance art with his styles and acts widely copied by other circuses and performers, including Batty and Fanque. Key to his success were his many talents — animal trainer, contortionist and equiliberalist, tightrope walker, poseur, choreographer, costume designer and equestrian. Above all he inspired others to, as Batty termed them in his advertisements in Ireland throughout 1841, "Equestrian Dreams of Wonder".

1   Handbill distributed by Astley — cited in Rendell, M. (2014) *Astley's Circus: The Story of an English Hussar*

2   *Norfolk Chronicle* — 5 October 1776 p.3.

3   *Ibid.* — 26 October 1776 p.2.

4   *Derby Mercury* — 9 October 1761 p.4. —
"Mr. JOHNSON,
Will Exhibit on *Friday, Saturday, Monday, and Tuesday*, being the 16th, 17th, 19th, and 20th of this Instant *October*, and absolutely no longer, (if the Weather permit) in a Close belonging to *Gilbert Oakes*, at the Top of *Green-Lane*,
' His Inimitable PERFORMANCES on HORSEBACK.
1st, He rides upon the Back of One Horse, standing on one Leg, and in that Position he gallops three Times round the Place;
2d, He rides Two Horses with his Foot-in each Inside Stirrup, and when the Horses are in full Speed, leaps from the Stirrups with a Foot upon each Saddle, and in that Posture continues toffing up his Cap, and cracking his Whip.
3d, He rides Three Horses, with a Foot upon each outside Horse, and when they are in full Speed, lets Two of them go, and leaps on the Third, without checking them.
4th, He rides a single Horse, and while in full speed mounts and dismounts instantaneously; and to the great Surprise of the Spectators, flies over the Horse when at his greatest Rates.
*Tho' what is here mentioned may seem incredible to those who have not seen Mr. Johnson, yet it is undoubtedly true, That his Performances exceed all Description. The Doors to be opened at Two in the Afternoon each Day, and mount exactly at Three. Admittance One Shilling each.*"

5   *A New Method and Extraordinary Method to Dress Horses* by William Cavendish, Duke of Newcastle, was published in 1667 and often reprinted for the next 150 years.

6   This was installed in 1818.

7   Burlettas were musical dramas characterised by rhymed lyrics and comic songs.

8   *Illustrated London News* — 17 May 1845 p.320.

9   *Edinburgh Evening Courant* — 24 January 1828 p.3.

10  *Ibid.* — 28 January 1828 p.3.

11  *North Wales Chronicle* — 17 February 1835 p.4.

12  British Museum playbills 170 — cited in Saxon, A.H. (1978) *The Life and Art of Andrew Ducrow & The Romantic Age of English Circus.*

13  *The Era* — 21 July 1839 p.6.

14  *Ibid.* 8 — 13 March 1847 p.173.

15  Wallett, W. F. (1884) *The Public Life of W. F. Wallett, the Queen's Jester: An Autobiography of Forty Years Professional Experience & Travels in the United Kingdom, The United States of America (including California), Canada, South America, Mexico and the West Indies.*

16  Certainly Pablo is mentioned as "Conductor of the Circle" in an advertisement placed for Batty's Circus Royal in the local press — *Oxford University and City Herald* — 24 July 1841 p.2.

17  *Ibid.* 15 p.70. — "Batty started for London by the first steamer, made arrangements to rebuild Astley's Theatre, and returned to Dublin in great exultation."

18  *Sunday Times* — 2 March 1851.

4

# Pablo is Coming!

*All you who are going to Donnybrook Fair,*
*Bear in mind that Pablo Fanque will be there,*
*With his Riders, his Horses, his Ponies and Clown,*
*To be seen for One Shilling what's worth Half-a-Crown —*
*For such wondrous feats sure never were seen,*
*Since a Fair was first held on famed Donnybrook Green.*

Dublin Weekly Nation — 24 August 1850

There is no account, apart from Wallett's autobiography[1] that records Pablo's decision to start his own circus. Wallett says:

It was my last night at the circus, and also that of Pablo, who left Batty to start an establishment of his own, which, after chequered fortunes, he still maintains.

After leaving Oxford, I went to Wakefield, Yorkshire, to join Pablo Fanque, who had erected a fine circus in Wood Street.[2]

It may have been Wallett himself that encouraged him to start out alone, for he also started his own circus at a later date[3], and had been put in charge of Batty's troupe in Dublin when he left for London. Fanque's motives however are unknown. The newspaper record suggests that he did not set up immediately on leaving Batty's. When Pablo left Oxford he was engaged at other establishments, with his son, and the decision was not made until later that year. In October 1841, he was at the Royal Amphitheatre in Liverpool, where the Liverpool Mercury stated:

The extraordinary Jumping of Mons. Pablo Fanque, through hoops covered with paper and encircled with knives, over high garters, and over nine horses was deservedly applauded ...[4]

The advertisement for the performance on the 11 October also mentions Master Pablo Fanque and that "Mr. Pablo Fanque will introduce his highly-trained Horse Xanthus"[5]. The Mercury, the next week, reported of the performance:

> The operations of the Persian horse Xanthes, on the "light fantastic toe", are truly astonishing, and reflect great credit on the gentleman under whose training he has attained such perfection. The evolutions performed on the corde volante, by Mr. Pablo Fanque were received with great applause, and very deservedly.[6]

Pablo and his son were next engaged at the Queen's Theatre, Spring Gardens, Manchester. In January 1842, we come across the first report of him erecting his own circus on Newton Street, Warrington:

> Not withstanding the badness of the times, Pablo Fanque, an equestrian formerly belonging to Batty's establishment, has had the courage to venture upon the erection of a circus in Newton-street, Warrington. Monday last was his opening night, and it is with considerable pleasure we have to record that the house was crowded to the ceiling, and that there could have not been much less than one thousand present. The amusements offered to their notice comprised the usual scenes in the circle, the principal performers being Pablo Fanque, his son, a child stated in the bills to be only nine years old, and Master Bill, a youth of very considerable promise. The feats displayed by Mr. Meeranardo, the modern Sampson, and other artists, under the names of the Wrestlers of Persia, with Bell and Fuller as clowns, were in high favour with the "gods", and everything passed off in a manner that will leave no room for the inhabitants of Warrington, or the proprietor, to regret his visit to our town.[7]

In March he was in Bridge Street, Chester, boosting receipts by making a donation to a local 'racing fund'[8], and by the end of May, Preston. His advertisement in the Preston Chronicle provides an insight into his circus programme, a mixture of the usual acrobatics, clowning, horsemanship and pantomime:

# PABLO FANQUE'S CIRCUS
## IN THE ORCHARD.

# NIGHTLY OVERFLOWS!
## SECOND GRAND CHANGE OF PERFORMANCE,
## ON MONDAY, TUESDAY, AND WEDNESDAY,

MAY, 30th and 31st, and JUNE 1st, 1842

# MR PABLO FANQUE

RESPECTFULLY informs the Inhabitants of Preston and Vicinity, that
the Circus has been fitted up with every attention to comfort, having been
thoroughly lined, — particularly the Boxes, every crevice being stopped,
to prevent draughts, and fitted up with taste; in short, every care has been
taken to render the place as comfortable as possible, the Proprietor having
spared neither pains nor expense to ensure him patronage and support.
A separate Private Entrance has been erected to the Boxes, Side Boxes, and Pit.
It is Mr. P.F.'s intention to give the proceeds of one night to some Charitable
Institution in Preston; due notice will be given.

## PROGRAMME OF PERFORMANCES.

1st. Mr. Pablo Fanque's intricate Leaping over a number of
difficult objects.

2nd. First of May; or Frolics of Cupid in the Soot Bag, Master
Pablo Fanque.

3rd. Two Nondescripts — Messrs. Griffiths and Heath.

4th. Principal Acts of Horsemanship — Mr Moffatt.

5th. Statues of the Ancients — Messrs. Smith and Taylor.

6th. Horseman of all work — Mr. Pablo Fanque

7th. Corde Floxo — Mr. H. Walker.

8th. Serious Pantomime — Three Fingered Jack — Mr. Moffatt
and the whole Company.

9th. Tight Rope — Master Pablo Fanque.

10th. Merry Millers; or, Old Grub's Wedding Day.

Boxes, 2s.; Side do., 1s.; Pit, 6d.; Gallery, 3d.

Sole Proprietor, Mr. PABLO FANQUE; Riding Master and Acting
Manager, Mr. MOFFATT; Clowns, Messrs. KEMP and GRIFFITHS.

For the accommodation of Families and Country Visitors, a
GRAND PERFORMANCE will take place on SATURDAY, JUNE
4th, commencing at two o'clock.[9]

The 1840s was a growth period for the provincial circus. Better established proprietors, such as the Cooke family, were either building or had previously built wooden, or, in some cases, brick amphitheatres in major towns, such as Hull, Glasgow, Perth, Liverpool, Manchester and Bristol. For example, The Royal Amphitheatre in Charlotte Street, Liverpool, where Pablo performed in 1841, was originally Cooke's New Circus. Opened in February 1826, it could accommodate 4000 people. In 1840, it became Ducrow's Royal Amphitheatre and was one of the many he ran as part of his business. These buildings were readily available for hire to those wishing to establish themselves, but wooden structures were also constructed on open ground in the growing industrial towns. In Preston, 'The Orchard', or 'Chadwick's Orchard'[10], was near the centre of the town and in the description given by Fanque he was at pains to point out that the building he constructed was both warm and comfortable. This belied the fact that the temporary nature of these buildings was just that. Many were poorly constructed and the cause of many accidents. In Great Yarmouth, for instance, Cooke's circus building, described as a "commodious and convenient building"[11] was the scene of an accident in 1845:

*Accident* — On Monday evening last, an accident occurred at Cooke's Circus, in the 2nd act of 'St George and the Dragon,' in consequence of the gallery being so crowded that a number of persons ventured themselves on the boarding thrown over the avenue leading to the stables; this not being sufficiently strong to bear so great a weight, broke down with a tremendous crash. We are happy to say, that only one person was seriously injured, a man named William Lilly, aged 53, who had his leg broken in two places. Mr. Cooke immediately sent for a fly[12], which conveyed him to the Hospital, and we are happy to state that he is, under the hands of Mr. F. Palmer, doing well.[13]

On 19 March 1848 however, Pablo's wife, Susannah was not so fortunate while the circus was in Leeds.

**FATAL ACCIDENT AT THE CIRCUS. KING CHARLES'S CROFT. ...**

On Saturday night last, a most awful scene occurred at Pablo Fanque's equestrian establishment, caused by the giving way of a beam supporting the pit and gallery, by which, about 600 persons were hurled to the ground. The place throughout was crammed to excess; but more especially this part of the house. The source of attraction on that evening was Mr. Wallett, the clown, who is a decided favourite in this quarter; and everything, up to a quarter to ten o'clock had proceeded favourably, when a slight cracking was heard in the pit and gallery, which caused such alarm to the people in that part of the building that they rose simultaneously. They had no sooner done this than the whole fabric gave way, which was caused in a great measure by the sudden change of position, and the greater portion of them fell below, those at the top of the pit having a considerable distance to travel. Everything was now changed from mirth to confusion; and to render this state of things doubly bad the greater part of the lights went out. Shrieks and screams were heard from the disabled; the people in the other parts of the house were clinging to posts, expecting their turn next; others swooning under fear and excitement; and those who were more collected, searching anxiously for a place of egress, for the door which had given them admittance was completely barricaded by the fallen timber. The gases, however, were soon lit again, and every assistance was rendered by those connected with the establishment to relieve the people amongst the ruins who were injuring each other.[14]

Fanque's wife, together with Mrs. Wallett, was at the cash desk directly under the part of the structure that fell. Wallett records in his autobiography:

My wife and Mrs. Pablo were seated together in the pay office beneath the falling mass. Mrs. Wallett happened to be sitting upright, and was knocked down by the timbers. She received some injury, but was not dangerously hurt. But poor Mrs. Pablo, who was looking over the front of the money-taking place, was struck by a falling beam, and killed on the spot. In the confusion that followed, some vile thief stole her watch from her side, and her box containing upwards of £50, the takings of the evening.[15]

At the subsequent inquest, Pablo claimed in his evidence that:

He rented the circus of a man named Britton. His wife was in the lobby taking cash, which is at the centre of the place where the accident occurred. It was near ten o'clock. He could not tell exactly what number of persons the place was capable of holding; but he thought they had more money in the gallery than on any previous occasion, although not so much taking it throughout. It was for the benefit of Mr. Wallett, on the Saturday night, when this took place, and the house was full. He had no reason to suppose that the building was insecure; it was down on one side. It was the side near to Lands-lane that was the lowest; but he was given to understand, on making inquiries, that it was in a leaning position when first erected, it had never shown previous symptoms of giving way. He believed it to be perfectly safe, or he would never have placed his wife in the lobby. ... It was the upper part of the pit that gave way. The circus was not built on his principle. He had erected similar places for upwards of six years; and had not had even a seat given way. He could not speak to the building being safe, although he entered it under the impression that it was perfectly secure, or he would never have trusted his wife and family in it. His architect preceded him for the purpose of inspecting the building; and he left it to him to make all necessary repairs. There were not separate beamings, so if one part gave way, the whole would come down. This concluded the substance of his evidence. The witness throughout was deeply affected and wept bitterly.[16]

A further witness stated that props should have supported the beams holding the gallery and pit, but they were missing. Mr. Britton, the original builder, was called to the witness stand. He gave evidence that the building had been originally constructed for Hengler's Circus, but had been rented for other uses since, including storage. He reported that it had been built to Mr. Charles Hengler's specification and these included supporting props in its design. It would seem that a previous tenant had removed the central props to create more space for goods that were being stored there. The coroner summed up by saying, "Although there was evidently a want of judgment in the matter, it did not appear to turn that any intentional neglect could be attached to any one" and instructed the jury to return a verdict of Accidental Death[17], which they did.

Susannah's body was laid to rest in Woodford Cemetery, Leeds, the following Wednesday:

The funeral *cortége* was of a very imposing character. The hearse was drawn by four cream-coloured horses. After the hearse followed the favourite horse of the deceased led by a groom. Then came the mourning coaches, and after them the whole of Pablo Fanque's stud of horses, bearing emblems of mourning, each led by a groom. The event appeared to excite great interest, and an immense concourse of people, amounting to at least 10,000, attended to witness the funeral.[18]

By the Monday, the troupe had moved on to their next engagement in Rotherham, and then on to Sheffield and the Knott Mill Fair in Manchester. On 16 May, Fanque married Elizabeth Corker[19], an equestrienne.

Whatever the public show of family unity, Fanque's family life must have been complicated. There is scant evidence that William Darby was officially married to Susannah Marlow, and it is very likely he had fathered a child with Maria Banham in Norwich when he was 18. The boy, William Darby Banham[20], aged 20 on the death of Susannah, was his apprentice and went under the name of Pablo Fanque Jun. The week before the accident, he had run-away causing Pablo to place an advertisement in the local press:

NOTICE TO CIRCUS MANAGERS AND OTHERS – ABSCONDED, on Monday, March 13th 1848, an APPRENTICE of Mr. Pablo Fanque's answering to the name of PABLO FANQUE, Jun., or MASTER BURKHAM [sic]. Notice is hereby given, that any Person or Persons Employing the said Youth after this notice will be Prosecuted according to the Law.

PABLO FANQUE
Circus Royal, March 13th, 1848, King Charles Croft, Leeds.[21]

Pablo Fanque Jun. was to abscond again in July 1849[22]. It seems this was a trait he never lost, as William Banham was later to desert his wife, Jane[23]. Emigrating to Australia, he took the name Pablo Fanque for himself and carved out a successful circus career. He died on 5 June 1869 in Sydney, New South Wales[24].

Susannah had two children by Fanque. William, born around 1832, and Lionel, born in 1836. It was Lionel who probably performed with his father as Master Pablo Fanque, but one cannot be certain of these family relationships or who was performing, given the cross-over of names. Indeed, following his father's marriage to Elizabeth, Lionel left the troupe, aged 12, to make his own way[25].

By the end of the 1840s it is clear that Fanque's circus had grown both in stature and popularity in the working towns of the north. There were some forays back to Norwich, but he rarely ventured into the territory of the large circus establishments, such as Batty's or the Cookes' — London, Dublin, Bristol, Glasgow or Edinburgh. This was to change in 1850 when he sought to expand, by seeking investment capital from Batty and Richard Bullard, the Norwich brewer.

Richard Bullard's interest in equestrian entertainment is relatively un-documented. It's clear he invested heavily in both Batty and Fanque during this period. In 1851, he certainly helped finance Batty's latest venture, The Royal Hippodrome, with the express aim of attracting audiences from the nearby Crystal Palace and Great Exhibition. The London Illustrated News reported:

WITHIN five minutes' walk of the Crystal Palace, Mr. Batty has erected a novel kind of circus, calculated to be a rival to his own Astley's, but for the difference of locality and aim. Opposite the Broad-walk, Kensington Gardens, an amphitheatre of enormous dimensions, under the title of "the Hippodrome," attracts all lovers of horsemanship. It consists of a circle of boxes and stalls divided by two opposite orchestra stations, which are occupied by two brass bands, who continue playing during the performance and an hour previous. The seats for the audience are covered, but the arena for Equestrian exhibition is open to the air and sky. We are thus carried back to the ancient times of Greece and Rome, and our own Elizabethan era; and the entertainments are suitable to these classical associations. Tournaments, chariot races, Trojan youths and Thessalian steeds, and such reproductions from the days of old, are the prevailing amusements. We believe, indeed, that the bills attempt no delusion in stating, that these exercises are "on a scale of extent and grandeur hitherto unattempted in England." The artists have been drafted from the Hippodrome at Paris, the principal being M. Louis Soullier, equerry to his Highness the Sultan Medjid of Turkey and the Emperor of Russia, and "his

*Richard Bullard established his Anchor Brewery with James Watts in 1837 in Coslany. He invested in both Batty and Fanque's circuses.*

numerous and highly-trained stud of horses" to whom may be added his company. The performance on Wednesday commenced with a pageant representing the meeting of Henry VIII. and Francis I. on the Field of the Cloth of Gold... The second part was not less interesting. The Brazilian coursers, performed by the three brothers Debach, on four horses each, was a highly exciting scene - presenting a trial of skill emulously carried out. But this was exceeded in interest by that exhibited by three female competitors, in a grand chariot race. The performances concluded with a monkey riding and driving four ponies; dames of the chase, in characteristic costume, on leaping palfreys; M. Frantz Debach, on the glove arienne, a well-known but difficult feat, and in this instance executed with inimitable grace; and the Corso races by Barbary coursers, as exhibition at the Carnival of Rome. We have omitted to mention an exceedingly amusing race by two ostriches of the desert, with their Arab riders, one of whom was thrown in the experiment.

The Hippodrome opened in May 1851, and in July Bullard was presented with a "massive gold snuff box of exquisite handcraft" by Batty's performers at Astley's and the Hippodrome[26]. This did not go un-noticed by the satirical columnist of "London Chit-chat" syndicated across the country:

A person, then, nearly as important as "The Cockney"[27] is a Mr. Bullard of Norwich, who being, as he says, a gentleman of fortune, has gone snacks with Mr. Batty in building a shed at Kensington, where piebald [sic] horses gallop round a ring, and ladies with very fresh colours and the shiniest of petticoats jump through hoops. Mr. Bullard — beg pardon, Richard Bullard Esquire — has had such a snuff box presented to him for this; and there was *such* a meeting at a public-house on Westminster-bridge, and *such* a reporting in the papers; and the poor devils who ride and jump, and draw salaries at the Hippodrome, how they did bow and scrape, and butter up. Richard Bullard, Esquire, is almost worthy to be London lord mayor.[28]

In 1850, Darby borrowed £765 from Bullard and £460 from William Batty. He was to use this investment to book prestigious venues, such as the Amphitheatre, in Great Charlotte-street, Liverpool (Christmas 1849 through to February 1850) and to operate a second company at the Amphitheatre in Sheffield. He was also able to employ the experienced William D. Broadfoot, as Stage Manager at Liverpool, and therefore stage popular hippodramas, such as Mazappa, Blue Beard, Black Prince, The Steeple Chase, St George and the Dragon and Timor the Tartar[29]. Broadfoot had been Ducrow's and Batty's manager at Astley's and had written and directed many of his most successful productions. Fanque's season in Liverpool came to an end on 24 February and Fanque's arrangement with Batty may have involved the purchase of the horse, Beda[30]. Beda was introduced as his own for the first time at Moor Street, Birmingham the following week, under the auspices of Franconi's Cirque National de France[31].

With an injection of capital Fanque could now retain his licence in Sheffield (by now at the Adelphi) and take a large retinue to Ireland. Freeman's Journal describes the troupe as, "undoubtedly the largest and most talented Company in Europe"[32]. While the advertisement he placed in the Dublin Evening Post gives us a better idea of the size and ambition of his enterprise:

In later advertisements he was to point out to the citizens of Dublin, "If you are not already of it, bear this in mind, and pay a visit immediately, and you will there see executed some wondrous achievements that have not been attempted even by Ducrow or Batty, who were, until the present time, considered the *ne plus ultra* of the Equestrian art"[34]. Indeed the reporter from Freeman's Journal backed up this claim when he wrote:

We have not had, in fact, for a long period in Dublin, anything approaching to first-class equestrian performance. Since the time of Ducrow, and subsequently of Batty, the equestrian performers visiting Dublin were, for the most part, either small

---

## PABLO FANQUE's CIRCUS ROYAL
## MUSIC HALL, LOWER ABBEY-STREET

——————

### OPEN EVERY EVENING

——————

MR. PABLO FANQUE begs most respectfully to inform the Nobility, Gentry, and Public generally, that he had opened the above extensive Premises for a limited period, for the display of Equestrian and Gymnastic Performances, and he flatters himself that the Entertainments will prove him to be highly deserving of that Patronage which has hitherto awards by a Dublin audience to similar Establishments.
The Company consists of the leading British, American, and Continental Male and Female
EQUESTRIANS,
Vaulters, Dancers, Acrobats, Professors of Gymnasæ, and an extensive Corps de Ballet; together with a numerous staff of
INFANT ACTORS, &c.,
and a Stud of
FORTY HORSES AND PONIES,
which will appear in Entertainments that will be brought forward in rapid succession; and every possible means will be resorted to, in order to produce Magnificent Historical and Romantic Spectacles, Kingly Sports, Princely Cavalcades, Knightly Pageants, &c.
Doors Open at Half-past Six. Commence at Seven, precisely.[33]

---

and insufficient detachments drafted from the London circus, or minor travelling troupes, possessing few performers and fewer horses, and distinguished for little beyond the vulgarism, sameness, and bad taste of their presentations ... But this company of Mons. Pablo Fanque, in the extent and beauty of its stud, the richness of its appointments, and the numbers and talent of its performers, is quite a different affair, and constitutes an equestrian establishment not inferior to the London circus[35].

The reception in Dublin may have seemed to Fanque that he had realised his earlier ambition to imitate Batty. He was to have rave reviews at all the other towns during his Ireland tour that summer. At Waterford he emulated Batty by driving "14 horses in-hand through the city with as much ease as does the driver of a stage-coach manage four"[36] and at Limerick the theatre in Henry Street was converted into a circus for his month's stay[37]. At Donnybrook Fair, towards the end of August, as a portent of things to come, the troupe performed in a huge marquee, "capable of holding upwards of 2000 persons at one time"[38]. The acquisition of a tent meant that the circus could perform in more places and for shorter periods. Pablo was to retain it for the remainder of the season at Ennis, where he had to move fields due to it being so damp[39], then at Galway, where the marquee was "brilliantly Illuminated with Patent Gas in the evening"[40]. It was at Galway on 13 September that Elizabeth Darby gave birth to their first child, also named Elizabeth, after her mother[41]. The circus briefly returned to Henry Street, Limerick, where Mazeppa was revived[42], while an amphitheatre was being constructed on the site of the old

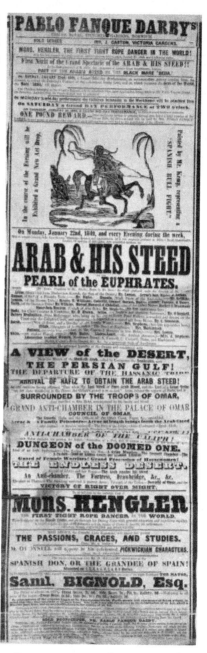

*Fanque returned to Norwich in 1849 with his Circus Royal, where Batty's Black Mare, Beda, performed.*

Theatre Royal in George Street, Cork ready for the winter season. The circus was to end its run in Cork on 21 January 1851, and returned to Dublin. On the last night in Dublin a conundrum competition was held with the grand prize of a pony, car and harness to the lucky winner. While competitions were a common occurrence in order to bring an audience in, the large prize drew particular interest with over a thousand entries:

## PABLO FANQUE'S CIRCUS ROYAL — CONUNDRUM NIGHT

Much amusement was afforded last night at the Circus, in Abbey-street by the competition amongst the wits of the city for a pony, car and harness which M. Pablo Fanque, following the example of the Wizard of the North, offered as the reward for the best original conundrum.

The value of the prize was estimated by Pablo Fanque at 30 guineas. The plan adopted for its adjudication was as follows: —

*Batty's Hippodrome was built in 1851 to attract crowds attending the Great Exhibition in 1851. It closed after the 1852 season and became a riding school.*

The audience selected from amongst themselves a jury of thirteen persons, none of whom were competitors, or were supposed to be acquainted with the facts that their friends had sent in conundrums. The jury nominated their own foreman, Mr. H. Ferguson, and 120 having been read, the jury retired to consider their verdict; and after the deliberation of an hour returned into court, declaring that No. 742 was, in their opinion, entitled to the prize. The following is the conundrum: — "Why is Mr. Pablo Fanque's Conundrum Prize of a Pony, Car and Harness, like a new-laid egg? Because there is a good j-oke in it."

The decision of the jury gave great dissatisfaction. They were assailed with exclamations of "Bribery" — "Corruption" — "We'll appeal to the Lords" — "We'll bring a question before the Court of Error!" Much disturbance ensued, and for some time a riot was threatened. Numbers of the audience leaped from the pit and lower gallery, and filled the Circus. Monsieur Pablo Fanque made his appearance in the midst of them, and was surrounded by a sea of rejected conundrums, which seemed disposed to engulf him and his prize pony. He addressed the audience, and intimated that the winner of the prize, (Miss Emma Stanley, of the Theatre Royal,) had not come forward to claim the prize [and] it would be sent to Dycer's upon the day, (Tuesday) to be sold by auction and the proceeds would be placed at the disposal of the Lord Mayor for the benefit of some local charity. Even this announcement did not pacify the indignation of disappointed genius, and for some minutes there was a pugilistic encounter of an alarming character. One of the officers of the establishment was cuffed, and he pummelled those around him in turn. The Circus was crowded by men, women, and children, rolling about in a great state of excitement and confusion. The police interposed and dispersed the disputants. One female was severely crushed, and fainted. The pony is a pretty cream-coloured animal, and the car and harness are in very good order. The jury had the power of considering the merit of each of 1,036 conundrums, and several besides the 120, beginning with the first in the book, were read for them and the audience. The proceedings terminated before 11 o'clock.[43]

Despite the unseemly end to Pablo's tour of Ireland, he had proved he could hold his own with the best of circus proprietors, establishing a reputation as a major player in the business. He was now ready to take on established circus families like the Cookes in their heartland, the Scottish cities of Edinburgh and Glasgow.

1  Wallett, W. F. (1884) The Public Life of W. F. Wallett, the Queen's Jester: An Autobiography of Forty Years Professional Experience & Travels in the United Kingdom, The United States of America (including California), Canada, South America, Mexico and the West Indies.
2  Ibid. p.74.
3  Ibid. p.86.
4  Liverpool Mercury — 8 October 1841 p.2.
5  Liverpool Mail — 9 October 1841 p.1.
6  Ibid. 4 p.6.
7  Manchester Courier and Lancashire General Advertiser — 8 January 1842 p.3.
8  Chester Chronicle — 25 March 1942 p.3.
9  Preston Chronicle — 28 May 1842 p.1.
10 The Orchard, from which the current street name derives, was the main open space in the town and where most outdoor events and annual fairs were held. In August of the same year a meeting at the Orchard, in which a rumour was circulated that a young girl had been killed in a Manchester mill (which in fact turned out to false), led to a riot. Loom workers attacked the mills in the town in an attempt to prevent the fires being stoked in preparation for the next morning's work. The military were called out and the riot act read. Five of the rioters were shot in the ensuing melée and two died from their wounds.
11 Norfolk Chronicle — 5 April 1845, p.3.
12 A fly was a four wheeled vehicle rather like a coach, which carried two inside passengers, but was drawn by two men instead of horses.
13 Ibid. 11.
14 Leeds Times — 25 March 1848 p.3.
15 Ibid. 1 p.75.
16 Ibid. 14.
17 Ibid. 14.
18 Leeds Mercury — 25 March 1848 p.5.
19 Ibid. 14 — 27 May 1848 p.8.
20 He was often described as Darby's nephew, but there is circumstantial evidence that he was the illegitimate son of Darby and Maria Banham. — see http://person.ancestry.co.uk/tree/82230404/person/38451196520/story, accessed 10 August 2016.
21 Ibid. 14 — 18 March 1848 p.5.
22 Sheffield Independent — 4 August 1849 — "RUN AWAY. — NOTICE TO EQUESTRIAN MANAGERS AND OTHERS/ WHEREAS, on the 30th ult., an Apprentice of Mr. Pablo Fanque Darby's Equestrian Establishment, has Absconded. He is supposed

to call himself Pablo Fanque Jun. Any Person that will give information that will lead to his detection, will be remunerated for their trouble ..."

23  Jane Banham was murdered in Armley in 1856, see *Liverpool Mercury* — 20 September 1856 p.6.

24  *Sydney Mercury* — 19 June 1869 p.2. — "PABLO FANQUE — Pablo Fanque, the most extraordinary, agile tight-rope dancer of the present age, died at his residence, Wilmot-street, Sydney, on Tuesday week last, the 8th instant, at the comparatively early age of 38. Pablo was a mulatio, though probably born in England. He was handsome, intelligent, well proportioned, vigorous man, who did not understand the meaning of the word fear. His performances in the Theatre Royal, shortly, after it was erected, about twelve years ago, will be remembered by a large proportion of the thousands who crowded nightly to see his extraordinary feats. Pablo had a wonderfully intelligent, well-trained black horse, which he named 'Wellington.' He brought his horse on stage, and caused him to perform some amusing tricks and dance the polka, but the cleverest feat of 'Wellington' was considered trifling in comparison to the least wonderful of those of his intrepid master. Pablo's line of Funambulism was not that of Blondin and Vertelli — he crossed no vast chasms or Cataracts on rope or wire, but his feats on a tight-rope passed from the stage to the dress circle were seldom equalled, and never surpassed by any other performer. He never made a false step in his various evolutions on the rope even when his feat were enveloped in bushel baskets, and he was in the practice of going the length of the rope throwing somersaults from the one end to the other, and alight and stand on one foot on the rope after the last somersault. When Pablo was here he had a good balance with his banker, and he subsequently was very successful in New Zealand, New South Wales, and Queensland. He appears to have retired into private life in consequence of ill-health prior to his decease. He died of consumption brought on by exposure to the elements during his professional perambulations."

25  *World's Fair* — 17 September 1932 cited in Turner, J.M. *Pablo Fanque, Black Circus Proprietor*, Black Victorians, Black Victoriana (2003) ed. Gerzina, G. p.26.

26  *London Evening Standard* — 25 July 1851 p.1.

27  The Mayor of London, often the butt of satirical jokes.

28  *Wells Journal* — 2 August 1851 p.5.

29  *The Era* — 17 February 1850 p.12.

30  Beda first appeared with Pablo Fanque in Norwich in January 1849, where she was "By the kind permission of W. Batty. Esq. proprietor of Astley's Royal Amphitheatre, London" — playbill "Pablo Fanque Darby's Circus Royal, Victoria Gardens, Norwich...Arab & his Steed or the Pearl of the Euphrates", Harry Ransom Center, The University of Texas at Austin.

31  *Birmingham Journal* — 23 February 1850 — "... upon which occasion M. PABLO FANQUE, the renowned Professor of Equitation, with his ENGLISH MARE, 'BEDA,' the gem of the World, will have the honour of appearing."

32  *Freeman's Journal* — 1 April 1850 p.1.

33  *Dublin Evening Post* — 4 April 1850 p.2.

34  *Ibid.* 31 — 11 April 1850 p.1.

35  *Ibid.* 31 — 22 April 1850 p.3.

36  *Waterford News* — 12 July 1850 p.2.
37  *Tralee Chronicle* — 3 August 1850 — "… which handsome arena has been converted into a circus, and fitted out in a style of splendour and magnificence, which reflects much credit on the enterprising and scientific proprietor, Mr. Joseph Fogerty, under whose superintendence the whole of the necessary alterations were completed, in the short space of ten days. The gallery has been constructed for accommodation of 1300 spectators, and the circle is 40 feet in diameter."
38  *Dublin Weekly Nation* — 24 August 1850 p.16.
39  *Clare Journal, and Ennis Advertiser* — 5 September 1850 p.3.
40  *Galway Vindicator, and Connaught Advertiser* — 11 September 1850 p.3.
41  *Ibid.* 32. — 17 September 1850 p.4.
42  *Limerick and Clare Examiner* — 19 October 1850 p.2.
43  *Dublin Evening Packet and Correspondent* — 25 March 1851 p.3.

# 5

# That perennial bankrupt Pablo Fanque

*Pablo Fanque, although well established in popular favour, succumbed to the internal weakness of a faulty or laggard management ...*

Charles W. Montague

Fanque's first foray into Scotland coincided with Glasgow's annual fair, which took place in July 1851, with his circus being by far the biggest attraction on the green. Pablo, in building his amphitheatre, mirrored the design of the best by including a stage. The Glasgow Herald remarked:

Next, we may notice M. Pablo Fanque's Circus, which is altogether the largest establishment of the kind which has ever set down in Glasgow; and certainly, in point of merit on the part of performers, is second to none we have seen in this city from the days of old Cooke down to Franconi. The stud is extensive, beautiful, and well trained, and the horsemen and horsewomen daring and agile in a high degree. Irrespective of the equestrian parts of the performance, there are various feats of strength and dexterity exhibited which have been rarely equalled. This establishment has, in addition to the ring, a dramatic stage on which some graceful and agreeable dances are performed. Everything is conducted, so far as we have seen, with decorum. The place is got up with great taste, and evidently at high cost, and as the price is such as to secure the exemption of sitting cheek-by-jowl with the young Red Republicans[1], such of our citizens as desire to pass an hour agreeably and innocently, may well patronise M. Pablo Fanque. Hitherto the establishment has boasted of bumper houses.[2]

William Darby must have been encouraged by his success when looking around the rest of the fair, perhaps remembering his origins and recalling the theatrical booths and minor circuses that he had been so attracted to in his youth. However, in doing so, he may have been oblivious to the widening opportunities for leisure and entertainment that were being presented to the working population, and the early signs of eventual decline of the annual fair as a focus for their patronage:

> The real observers of the Fair vibrate between the shows and the nearest public-house; but thousands wiser, and more economical, flock to the coast and inland parts of the country, to spend their day of leisure in a manner more befitting the age of steamboats and locomotives. ... There are a fair number of booths of minor importance, the attractions of which consist in performing hares, magic, a dwarf, and a fat lady! Oh how the pleasant days of youth are reviewed, by mention of these greatest wonders of the world; for disguise it from ourselves as we may, dwarfs, giants, and giantesses, and fat youths of both sexes, are woefully scarce, when compared to the days of our childhood.[3]

But for the time being at least, and despite the type of class that the fair seemed to attract, Pablo's circus was drawing in the right sort of clientele. Circus proprietors of the period craved a middle class, as well as a working class audience, and did all they could to engender both respectability and family values. As the season drew-on, as on other occasions, his mare Beda was the star of the circus, allowing others to admire her training and speculate of her worth:

> We are glad to observe that this attractive and well-conducted place of amusement is patronised by the public, as it deserves to be. During the fair holidays, the audiences were overwhelming. They are no less so now: but the visitors are generally of a higher class; and the boxes and pit exhibit a large sprinkling of West-end gentility. During the week there has been produced a spectacle of a most gorgeous kind, entitled the "Arab and his Steed, or the Pearl of the Euphrates." The piece embodies a very pretty eastern tale full of varied and exciting incidents, all of which are admirably brought out by M. Pablo Fanque's joint equestrian and dramatic

company; for it is a new and important feature in this establishment that it has a stage attached to it, the performers on which are of fully average merit, and the "scenery, dresses, and decorations," are excellent. An Arabian mare named "Beda," plays a prominent part in this Eastern piece, and we may truly say that the beauty and docility — we had almost added the intelligence — of this fine animal really extend to the marvellous. "Beda" undoubtedly exhibits a degree of training which we have never seen equalled in any other of her species. She is the envied of all fanciers of horse flesh, and we believe M. Fanque, were he disposed, could sell her at a price which would be enough to mount a troop of dragoons. We advise our readers to see this brilliant piece. The other performances are exceedingly lightsome and attractive; and indeed this Circus presents every thing the best of its kind. As a proof of the magnitude of the establishment, we may state that it embraces 160 individuals in its various departments, and the stud numbers 40 horses and ponies.[4]

Following a long stay in the city, Fanque moved for the winter season to Nicholson Street in Edinburgh, opening on 6 November. The Cooke family had been the first to construct an amphitheatre on this site, behind the York Hotel, in 1839. Pablo was keen to ensure he could at least equal or better their tradition:

M. Pablo Fanque who has acquired a high name in his profession, arrived in Edinburgh this week with his extensive establishment. The amphitheatre which he has erected for his company occupies the usual site of these fabrics behind the old York Hotel in Nicholson Street; and having been opened for the first time on Thursday evening, we shall briefly detail our impressions of the troupe.

The design of the Circus itself is elegant and striking, presenting an agreeable change from the style to which we have been accustomed. The spectators occupy three sides of the amphitheatre, having an excellent view both of the arena and of the stage. The "drop scene," which conceals the mysteries beyond, is a well-executed picture of a classical ruin; and the scenic effect is very fine. The house has three divisions — boxes, pit, and gallery; and rising in successive tiers, to some height, the interior has an impressive aspect. The panelling displays a series of paintings, which with the other decorations, impart a chaste and elegant appearance to the house. The arrangements for the comfort of spectators are at once liberal and complete.[5]

Pablo's next venue was the Manchester Free Trade Hall[6], and once again, no expense was spared in adapting the space to take the ring:

The accommodation in the Free-trade Hall is far superior to any which has yet been previously offered on similar occasions. The reserved seats, or dress circle, will be as usual on the platform; the second class immediately in front of the platform extending round to the right of the ring; at the extreme end of the hall an immense gallery, called the arena, has been raised on the incline, with backed seats, extending the whole width of the Hall, and advancing within a few feet of the ring; this alone will accommodate about eight hundred people; the promenade is to the left, and is so arranged that all the occupants will be enabled to have a fair observation of the performances. The entrance to the arena and promenade will be at the usual door for admission to the body of the hall, – those for the first and second class seats at the reserved seats door, nearest to Deansgate.[7]

William Darby's ambition was no doubt to elevate his establishment in the eyes of the public to match those of Batty, the Cookes and Ducrow. However, it is clear from the newspaper accounts of the time that neither Batty nor the Cookes had spent so extravagantly in these provincial towns and cities for some time. During this period, Batty confined his main activity to Astley's and his new Hipprodrome in London, as well as owning smaller travelling establishments, including a menagerie, which were run by managers. William Cooke's circus mostly operated in the southern towns – Brighton, Plymouth etc. with the odd foray as far north as Leeds. This meant there was little effective competition for Fanque in these years from these traditional British circuses. During the next decade, however, things were to change.

A threat came from a slow influx of American performers and circuses[8] making the journey across the Atlantic. Thomas Taplin Cooke had been the first to realise the potential of the American market by taking his troupe to the United States in 1839. However, by 1842, it was American circuses that were making the journey eastward to Britain and Europe. With the advent of steam, travel time between Liverpool and New York had become feasible for such enterprise. In 1838, The Great Western, one of the first cross-Atlantic steamships, made the voyage in 15.5 days, but between 1845 and 1850 the average time taken to cross the Atlantic dropped from 14 to 9.5 days. In addition, the size of liners increased substantially, with capacities of up to 1,500 passengers.

From 1842 onwards many of these American performers appeared in British theatres and circuses where managers were keen to provide the new American acts. John Aymar, for instance, made his appearance at the Royal Lyceum Theatre and Opera House in 1843 as part of "a New American Equestrian Company, wonderful Stud of American Horses, and talented Dramatic Company for the Metropolitan theatres ... Mr. L. I. North, the Star Rider of America. Mr. Aymar, Mr. Sands &c. &c. the elite of the American Equestrians. Talent, Splendour, Fun and Wonders"[9] where he was to "throw a back somersault on horseback"[10]. He was to then join Batty's troupe in Dublin, where Sanders News-Letter stated:

> ... imported last week the celebrated American performers, Messrs. E.O. Dale and Mr. Aymar ... The performances of these gentlemen surpass anything of the kind ever witnessed. The extraordinary summersaults by the first-named artist, as well as the riding and gymnastic displays by Mr. Aymar, are of the most extraordinary description, and withal elegant.[11]

He was to remain with Batty's until a tragic accident occurred in Jersey:

DREADFUL DEATH of Mr. AYMER, THE CELEBRATED VAULTER. — This unfortunate man, whose recent performance at the English Opera, under the management of Van Amburgh and Titus, excited so much admiration in his peculiar department, met his death on Thursday night at the Circus of Mr. Batty, proprietor of the Royal Amphitheatre, who has several establishments in various parts of the kingdom, and one in the island of Jersey, where the late performer was fulfilling an engagement. The particular performance for which Mr. Aymer was announced concluded with a double summerset, a feat considered almost (if not quite) impossible, and in throwing it the ill-fated artist, instead of alighting on his feet, fell on his neck, and death was the immediate result. Mr. Batty, on hearing the fatal intelligence yesterday morning, immediately quitted London for Jersey.[12]

It was American performers, already in the country, rather than incomers, that were to establish partnerships and bring US razzmatazz to the British circus. Chief among them was James Hernandez, who had first appeared at Astley's in 1849, and his partner Eaton Stone.

In April 1852, they hired Pablo Fanque's amphitheatre in Nicholson Street, Edinburgh:

PABLO FANQUE'S AMPHITHEATRE,
YORK HOTEL, NICHOLSON STREET, EDINBURGH,
Will Open on MONDAY, April 5, 1852,
For Twelve Nights only.

———

MESSRS WELCH[13] & Co., Proprietors of the GREAT AMERICAN EQUESTRIAN ESTABLISHMENT, beg respectfully to intimate to the Nobility, Gentry, and Citizens of Edinburgh, that, in consequence of *the courtesy of Mr. Pablo Fanque,* they will have the opportunity (before commencing their season in Birmingham) of appearing in the
NICHOLSON STREET AMPHITHEATRE
For a Short Season of positively only Twelve Nights.
The Splendid Practical Illustrations of the ART OF HORSEMANSHIP will introduce the following celebrated Performers:-
The Incomparable Horseman,
HERNANDEZ
The Wonder of the World.
Mr. EATON STONE
The Distinguished Indian Horseman of the Camanchees.
Mr HIRAM FRANKLIN
The Great Aerial Evolutionist.
Mr. ARTHUR NELSON
The Musical Momus.[14]

Despite their use of Pablo's amphitheatre in Edinburgh, Welch, Hernandez and Stone were soon to establish the American way of doing things, by purchasing a tent when they got to Birmingham:

---

WELCH, HERNANDEZ AND CO's
AMERICAN CIRCUS AND MAMMOTH MARQUEE,
with a talented company of American Equestrians, including the world-renowned Hernandez, Hiram Franklin, Eaton Stone, and a numerous troupe of auxiliaries will visit the following towns, entering in Grand Procession each day at Eleven o'Clock with their beautiful American Carriages and unrivalled Stud of Horses: - Tewkesbury, Monday, May 17; Cheltenham, 18 and 19th; Gloucester, 20; Stroud, 21; Wootton-under-Edge, 22.
Day performance at Two o'Clock; Evening performance at Half-past Seven.[15]

---

The use of a marquee established a fully peripatetic troupe, enabling the circus to abandon the expense of building or hiring expensive city and town amphitheatres. It also brought the circus to smaller rural towns and communities, without being tied to the round of annual fairs. When the circus arrived in Nottingham in November the local newspaper described the structure:

WELCH, HERNANDEZ, & CO.'S EQUESTRIAN COMPANY. — This American establishment, is now in Nottingham, and has this week been performing to most overflowing and delighted audiences. … The erection is termed "a portable Equestrian Palace," and is really a splendid pavilion, designed and manufactured by Mr. G. Griffin, tent maker, Birmingham. It is a novel one, having only been used once before, as we are informed, and that on the occasion of Prince Albert laying the foundation stone of a popular building. It is so constructed as to prevent the intrusion of damp and cold air, being suspended from the centre by strong elastic ropes; it is in stripes of brilliant scarlet and white, and being lighted by gas jets has a beautiful effect.[16]

By January 1853 Welch had withdrawn[17] and the circus was now under the control of Hernandez and Eaton Stone. In Halifax they were to find their tent no less vulnerable than traditional wooden circus buildings:

## HALIFAX

A CIRCUS BURNT DOWN. — The American Tent Circus under the management of Messrs. Hernandez and Stone was pitched in Cadney's Croft on Monday week, and the equestrians have had the satisfaction of performing to crowded houses every night since their arrival, although up to Sunday the weather has been very unfavourable, on account of the rain. On Monday there was a change in the weather, the day being dry and frosty, and the usual performance took place in the American pavilion. After the performance, and after all parties had left the place, save three men who were sleeping in that part of the pavilion known as the dressing room, a fire broke out. It appears that a fire had been kept, as is usual, in the dressing room, and at about half-past one o'clock on Tuesday morning, the three men were awoke by the cry of "Fire, fire." Some part of the dressing room had been ignited, and in consequence of the previous dry frosty day, the pavilion was in a good condition for a blaze. In less than half an hour the whole of the top canvas was consumed, as were also the dresses, robes, &c. The seats and chairs were only partly damaged. The fire could not have happened more unluckily, as Tuesday night was a bespoke one, under the patronage of Colonel Pollard, and the 2nd West Yorkshire Cavalry Band was to be in attendance. It is stated that Messrs. Hernandez and Stone will sustain a loss of upwards of £600, the tent being of the best kind, and having only been in use two or three months.[18]

Despite this setback, by the following month, the tent had been repaired and they were performing in Manchester. Within a year, however, the tent had been abandoned and another partner had been taken on, becoming Hernandez, Stone & Newsome's[19] American Circus. By January 1855 they had hired the Victoria Riding School in Bath where, "... the interior has been converted into stalls, boxes, side-boxes, and a promenade lounge, besides the usual pit and gallery. The posts have become pillars, the fronts of the boxes panelled, the roof is covered with a white ceiling, globe lamps diffuse a mellow light, and in short, the building, instead of presenting the raw, unfinished temporary character to which we are accustomed, has assumed the appearance of a permanent, neat, and even elegant circus. Then, again, admirable arrangements have been made for the comfort of visitors in easy staircases, cushioned seats, and carpeted floors. We may illustrate the excellent style which pervades, the establishment, from the most prominent to the minutest point, by stating the ring itself is *carpeted*."[20]

By February the partnership had been dissolved and the bulk of the travelling circus purchased by entertainment entrepreneur E.T. Smith. [21]

Smith[22] had been the licensee of the Marylebone Theatre, but in 1852 took on the licence for the Theatre Royal, Drury Lane. In doing so he probably saved it from demolition by introducing a mixed programme of traditional drama and a circus season[23]. In purchasing his own circus, run by managers, he could also maintain a touring troupe.

By the end of 1854, Fanque had effectively lost control of his own business. Richard Bullard's remaining investment in Darby had been taken over by William Batty, and while Pablo was at Worcester in December of that year, he decided to call it in[24]. The circus was sold at auction and, with no bidders, Batty bought it for £500. In an arrangement unbeknown to others, Fanque was to rent his own circus back from Batty[25].

In February 1855, together with E.T. Smith's newly acquired troupe, he visited Manchester again. From the description in the Manchester Times the combination of the two troupes provided mutual benefit:

THE CIRCUS, FOUNTAIN-STREET. — This place of amusement opened for the season on Saturday last, under the direction of E.T Smith, lessee of the Drury Lane Theatre, who brings to us an extensive company and considerable talent. The success which Mr. Smith has attained in the management of the great national establishment will, no doubt, give him a certain *prestige* in Manchester, but his treasury will only be made safe by talent and successful novelties. This, it appears, the manager is preparing for his patrons, as will be seen on reference to our advertising columns. The present company is announced in it, which proved so successful at Drury Lane Theatre, in conjunction with

Pablo Fanque's troupe, and is, consequently, not only strong in a numerical point of view, being able to present to the public a greater range and variety than is usual, but equally so in talent, witnessed from the evident approval of the audience, as evinced by continued applause throughout the evening, and the frequent recalls of the principal performers. We may venture to predict that the chances are in favour of the proprietor, E.T. Smith, meeting with the support of the Manchester people which is necessary to the carrying out of his speculation in a manner satisfactory to himself as well as to the public.[26]

However, significant competition was to come from America[27] when Howes and Cushing United States Circus arrived in March 1857. Their announcement in the Manchester Times clearly proclaimed their intention:

**HOWES AND CUSHING'S**
**GREAT UNITED STATES CIRCUS**
The Largest Establishment in the World, numbering nearly
200 MEN AND HORSES,
Comprising exclusively of American Equestrian and
Gymnastic Artists,
AMERICAN HORSES, AMERICAN CARRIAGES AND
HARNESS,
And a full American Equipage generally;
...

————

**THE IMMENSE CANVAS AMPHITHEATRE**
In which the company give their entertainment is of a circular form, 450 feet in circumference, and occupies a space covering nearly half an acre of ground. The canopy is supported by sixteen masts, from the peaks of which are displayed the national banners of various countries. Seats are constructed for the accommodation of
5,000 SPECTATORS
and the whole enclosure is brilliantly illuminated with gas, manufactured on the ground, in portable apparatus.[28]

To the outside world, by the time Howes and Cushing had arrived in Britain, Pablo's business seemed to be successful, but there were signs that all was not well. In April 1858, Fanque was taken to court by Arthur Nelson, the Clown, for non-payment of his salary while appearing at Bristol from September to February 1857. Nelson had been engaged at a salary of £7 a week and claimed he had not been paid from 31ˢᵗ October to when he left in February, a period of 17 weeks. The judge deemed that, "the way in which Mr. Manager Taylor kept the pay sheets as to the troupe's salaries, was neither clear or satisfactory. He said he had no regular account book; and Nelson said in Court that he, Taylor, did not know when he left Mr. Fanque's service or what balance was due him the clown. ... Thus the verdict went in the clown plaintiff's favour"[29].

In September 1858 the circus was seized[30] in Harrogate, and a bankruptcy notice served against Fanque in October.

At the Leeds court of bankruptcy, which local newspapers described as "stormy", the main claimant was B. Foster of Wakefield, a carrier employed to move the circus from one venue to another. However, others now came forward to prove claims against the assets. The amount totalled £606 9s 11d.[31] The following month, "the entire and extensive and valuable WARDROBE, SCENERY, DECORATIONS, Appurtenances, Paraphernalia, Tent and Fittings, and other Effects, lately used in the equestrian establishment of the above bankrupt"[32] were to be sold by auction after the Leeds fair. However, the circumstances were clearly complicated, as by December, we learn that Fanque's last examination in court had been postponed until 31 January. The debts now amounted to £2,900 and "the assets will not pay the expenses, the greater part of the bankrupt's effects having been swept off, under an execution, by Mr. Battye [sic], the proprietor of Astley's Amphitheatre, London"[33]. Indeed it was William Batty again, not Forster, that had seized the circus in Harrogate, and the delay in settling the debts to creditors had come about because the balance sheet, which "extended over 100 pages"[34], made no mention of any transactions with Batty. The Commissioner adjourned the examination until Batty himself could appear and Pablo was ordered to submit revised accounts concerning these transactions.

On the 15 January the court re-convened. First, it was stated that, Batty had seized the circus at Worcester in 1854. It was then revealed that, "immediately after the seizure at Worcester, in fact the same night, allowed the bankrupt the use of his establishment for a payment of £10 a week — about £500 a year"[35]. In response to the order to submit revised accounts, Mr. Barwick, acting for Fanque, told the court that "he had kept no books, and had furnished the best account he could under the circumstances"[36]. Indeed, according to the *Era*, Fanque, in order to retain his means of livelihood four years previously, had sold "twelve horses, five ponies, a number of carriages lent, equestrian dresses, properties &c. for £500"[37] to Batty and hired them back at a cumulative cost of £2500 in the years subsequent to the sale. The court was once again adjourned until Batty could be present to verify these transactions. In the meantime, Fanque had appeared at Liverpool[38] and Glasgow[39] with his horse Beda, but was now forced to attempt to sell her[40].

Finally, in June, time ran out for Pablo with the most condemning of results:

PABLO FANQUE IN THE BANKRUPTCY COURT. — On Monday, in the Leeds Court of Bankruptcy, Mr. Commissioner Ayrton delivered judgment as to the certificate of William Darby (Pablo Fanque), the well-known equestrian manager. The accounts in the balance-sheet, the Commissioner observed, extended over twenty-two months, from January 1857, to September 1858, and there was a deficiency of £438. The debts were £2,765, and the assets £165, so that there would be no dividend whatever. The bankrupt had kept no books. For some years past he has apparently been the owner of a large equestrian establishment, but it now appeared that a person named Battye was the real owner, the entire establishment being hired of him by the bankrupt. ... that there were no books to test the accounts, which were unsatisfactory; that the bankrupt had been guilty of perjury in an affidavit; and that the debt owed to Mr. Myers[41] was incurred fraudulently. As to the transactions with Battye they certainly were of a singular character, and calculated to arouse suspicion, but it was sufficient for him (the Commissioner) to say that nothing fraudulent had been proved before him ... nor did he think the bankrupt had been guilty of such misconduct in regard to the keeping of books as a call for punishment. The next charge was a very serious one — that of perjury. ... the latter had made an affidavit in which he swore that he had an equestrian establishment worth £1,000 after payment of all liabilities. … the affidavit was important, in order to test the bankrupt's character for veracity. Unfortunately for the bankrupt's character, it was too clear that the affidavit was intended to deceive. The statement that the establishment was worth £1,000, and was his property, was utterly untrue … it was clear therefore, that the bankrupt had been guilty of perjury. It appeared that Mr. Myers was about to advance money to the bankrupt and on applying for security he was told that Battye had power over everything except a certain mare called Beda, and the bankrupt excused himself from giving her as security on the ground that he had sworn on oath to his wife never to give it for security. On this representation the debt was contracted, and Mr. Myers forbore to insist on having the security. Mr. Myers stated in his evidence that if he had known that the mare did not belong to the bankrupt, he would not have allowed him to have the money. It appeared, in fact, that at this time the mare in question was the property of Mr. Battye, and that the bankrupt's story was untrue. The bankrupt denied this statement, but there was no reason to doubt the veracity of Mr. Myers, or Mr. Marshall, his solicitor, who confirmed this statement, while the bankrupt had shown that no reliance could be placed on his word.[42]

The true ownership of Pablo's circus was to be tested in the Court of Exchequer on 24 June when a case was brought against Batty to determine whether he was the official assignee[43] of William Darby. The account by Batty's barrister in court sheds a great deal of light on the true nature of the arrangement:

About 17 or 18 years ago he [Batty] became acquainted with William Darby, then a lad, and took him as apprentice, and when Darby's apprenticeship had expired he commenced business as an equestrian on his own account, and travelled about the country with a circus under the name Pablo Fanque. In 1850 he became indebted to a Mr. Buller in a sum of 765l., and to Mr. Batty in another sum of 460l. for money advanced, making a total sum of 1225l., for which he gave them a joint bill of sale on his property, and also a warrant of attorney as collateral security. Mr. Batty, then undertook the financial management of the establishment, and the surplus receipts were regularly transmitted to him, and were applied to the liquidation of the debt. The bill of sale was afterwards lost by the person in whose custody it had been placed; but in 1854, Mr. Batty having made further advances to Pablo, and the concern not being so flourishing as it had previously been, it was thought necessary to have another bill of sale, and one was accordingly executed; but that was destroyed in consequence of its existence being no longer necessary. In November 1854, Mr. Buller's debt was reduced to a small sum by payments, and Mr. Batty having undertaken to pay the balance, the whole securities were handed over to him; shortly afterwards Mr. Batty put the bill of sale into force, and had the circus and all the property put up for sale by auction in one lot at Worcester, and there being no bidder for a higher sum than 500l., he himself became the purchaser. He, however, allowed Pablo to carry on the business of the circus as before, charging him a certain sum per week for rent, and this arrangement continued up to the time when the property was seized under the bankruptcy.[44]

Fanque's friend William Wallett, in his later autobiography, put his financial downfall squarely on the shoulders of William Batty:

From Birmingham I went to Kidderminster, and took the management for Mr. Pablo. At Worcester I obtained possession of the splendid hall, and fitted it up as an elegant circus. I formed a magnificent ring. The horses ran on a cocoa-nut pile matting, the centre of the arena being covered with Brussels carpet, thereby avoiding the dust and dirt of the ordinary sawdust floor. The patronage bestowed upon us was unequalled in the history of Worcester; but notwithstanding the favour of the public, my ill luck again overtook me. For Batty came down, holding a bill of sale from Mr. Pablo, and in the most wanton and unfeeling manner sold up the whole concern. This ruined my friend Pablo, upset my arrangements, and for a time blighted my prospects. ... Now the whole property at Worcester had been sold in one lot, and bought by Batty, who arranged with Pablo to manage it as before. ... The evil genius of Batty marred everything.[45]

Wallett's dislike of Batty might well have clouded his judgment as he was perfectly aware of Pablo's shortcomings being one of the creditors, claiming he was owed £113 from Fanque's assets in 1858; a fact vehemently denied by Pablo.[46]

Having been declared bankrupt, and denounced as a perjurer in England, it would seem that Darby's plight could not have been worse. While it was clear that the English bankruptcy court could not touch any assets he might have in Scotland, creditors were circling there as well. He was subsequently declared bankrupt in Glasgow. In this instance, the creditors receiving 6d in the pound.[47]

Whatever Fanque's legal position, it would seem that bankruptcy in both England and Scotland did not dampen his enthusiasm. While undergoing bankruptcy in February, he not only presented a new horse, Lady Ayr, to the Glasgow public[48], but also attempted to publish a book on horse training.[49] His circus was certainly back on the road appearing in Blackburn by June.[50] By July, he was back in Burnley and could afford to employ six clowns, despite the fact that audiences were poor:

*William Wallett, clown and friend to Pablo Fanque.*

PABLO FANQUE'S CIRCUS. — During the week, the old favourite, Pablo Fanque, has been giving his celebrated performances in a large and commodious circus tent on a plot of ground at Fulledge. Two entertainments each day have generally been given, rather too often, we are inclined to think, when the stay is over a day, as may be judged from the fact of a very poor attendance up to last night. We are very sorry that Mr. Pablo has overlooked this. For as far as the performances go they can not [sic] be equalled, the

*In 1860, Fanque called his circus "Phoenix", after he had been declared bankrupt in England and Scotland.*

different artistes have been carefully selected, the majority of their feats are good and original, and elicited "thunders of applause." Mr. Pablo introduced his wonderful and beautiful mare, "Miss Nightingale or Lady Ayr," her performances are truly unprecedented. Six clowns contributed greatly to the fun of the entertainment. Last night under the patronage of Capt. Dugdale and the officers and members of the Burnley Rifle Corp. The corps mustered in uniform at Keighley Green and headed by the band proceeded to the circus. We earnestly wish Mr. Pablo success.[51]

One cannot but be a little suspicious of how quickly, and with relative ease, Fanque was able to re-establish his business. Following his visit to Burnley and Colne in July, he went on to Bradford, where he aptly named his circus, Phœnix[52]. There is no evidence of how he obtained the money to do so. One theory might be that Batty, or maybe Richard Bullard, had once again rescued Darby from oblivion. Clearly this is what had happened in 1850 and 1854. While Batty administered the debt to himself and Bullard in the early 1850s, his 'carelessness' in losing the bill of sale, and not taking a more active part in the day-to-day running of Pablo's business to protect his investment might suggest disinterest or tardiness at the very least. Batty retired from public life in 1853, having amassed a fortune, but was running touring troupes under his own name during this period, using managers. Why Pablo was allowed to retain his own name on the circus in 1854 one might never discover, but it might have been that his name or 'brand' was so strong that this unique arrangement was of benefit to Batty. Clearly the main creditors had their suspicions as to the financial arrangements between Batty and Darby otherwise they would not have attempted to appeal to the Court of Exchequer, which they did on November 1859[53].

Another theory can be based on a fact that emerged on Pablo's death. Newspapers reporting his death stated that, "he came into possession of £4,000., some years ago, on the death of a son in Australia"[54] (some accounts say an 'adopted' son[55]). Since this could only refer to William Darby Banham, who died much later in 1869, this conclusion is dubious, particularly as there is no evidence of Banham leaving a will in Australian probate records.

The most likely explanation lies in a partnership with another person willing to capitalise on his name. During the next eleven years this became a common trait. When Fanque could not finance a tour himself, he partnered with another showman, theatre licensee, or performer. Despite Darby's fall from grace it would seem that others were prepared to invest in Pablo's resurrection. Pablo's reputation among all classes was more than secure in the northern towns of England being a much loved and respected "caterer of public entertainment"[56]. It is this that may have enabled him to secure temporary investment time and time again.

He continued his circus, mainly tenting in the smaller industrial towns of Lancashire, around Manchester, remaining a stalwart at fairs and other traditional holiday gatherings throughout the region. Even during the Lancashire Cotton Famine of 1861-65[57], he maintained his presence in the region. The Leeds Times remarked in July 1862, concerning the town's mid-summer fair:

> The pleasure fair has not been as numerously attended as has been the case in times of prosperous trade, for the gloom which overhangs the commercial world of Lancashire has to some extent saddened the horizon under which our own industries are conducted. There

was a fair show of canvas theatres and circuses and Pablo Fanque - an old favourite in Leeds - has had his endeavours nightly rewarded by crowds of appreciative townsmen.[58]

There were brief forays outside this region. In 1863 he spent most of the summer season in the north-east having established a working partnership with Mr. Stanley, the proprietor of the Tyne Concert Hall in Newcastle, who had restored the building to its original circus configuration.[59] In 1866, he returned to Ireland, being ringmaster for Swallow's Circus, visiting once again the Abbey Street Amphitheatre[60] before partnering with Tom Barry in Cork[61].

Examining his itinerary during these years shows that at times his retinue was very small[62], hiring his skills and name to others, while concentrating on bringing on apprentices and actively seeking children to train in equestrianism[63].

*Pablo Fanque died at the Britannia Inn, Stockport.*

William Darby was to pass away at the Britannia Inn, Stockport on 5 May 1871[64]. Even in death he courted financial controversy. John Walker, a juggler in his circus, had lent him £5, which he required to be repaid, but Pablo had died suddenly. As a result he sued Elizabeth Darby, his widow and administratrix of the estate. In court, Elizabeth's barrister "asserted that the defendant had not a rag, her husband having died hopelessly insolvent. Sometime before his death, the deceased assigned every particle of his property, in consideration of a sum of £150 lent to him by a Mr. Knight, of Manchester, who had now taken possession of everything"[65]. In order to settle the case, her barrister paid the £5 out of his own pocket.

1   Used here to refer to the working class as a catch-all phrase. The "Red Republicans" were a political party during the 1848 revolution in France and espoused the ideas of Marx and Engels in their *Communist Manifesto* published that year. As the *Illustrated London News* put it, when referring to the revolution, "The Working classes or 'Red Republicans' were imbued with the doctrine of Communism. ... As a standard of this new creed, they raised the red flag. They called themselves Red Republicans, and those among them who were sincere looked for a social Millennium as the inevitable consequence of a Revolution founded upon their ideas." — *Illustrated London News* — 1 July 1848 p.415. In Britain, the *Red Republican* also referred to the title of a radical newspaper published by George Julian Harney in 1850. In its last issue in November 1850 it printed the first English translation of the *Communist Manifesto* re-titled, *Friend of the People*.

2   *Glasgow Herald* — 18 July 1851 p.5.

3   *Glasgow Sentinel* — 12 July 1851 p.5.

4   *Ibid.* 2 — 4 August p.5.

5   *Edinburgh Evening Courant* — 8 November 1851 p.2.

6   On the site of St. Peter's Fields, where the 1819 Peterloo Massacre took place, the building that the circus occupied would have been the simple brick structure built in 1843 to replace a wooden building constructed in 1840. It had capacity of 7000. The present listed building was built in 1853 and is now a hotel.

7   *Manchester Times* — 28 February 1852 p.5.

8   American circus troupes, while performing traditional equestrian acts, also brought their own popular culture to British audiences, in particular, blackface minstrels — "AMERICAN CIRCUS, ROYAL AMPHITHEATRE. A company of equestrians, recently arrived from the United States, made their first bow to an English auditory at the Amphitheatre last evening. The spacious building was crowded in every part long before the performances commenced. The shout of welcome which greeted the appearance of each candidate for British favour must have been highly gratifying to the recipients. The performances were admirably and almost faultlessly executed. We have only space to notice the racy and original negro singing of Mr. Sweeny, who accompanied himself on the banjo, or mandoline [sic]. His instrumentation is excellent, and his self-possession, while the house convulsed with laughter at his "niggerisms," was irresistibly comic. He was encored three times." — *Liverpool Mail* — 29 March 1842 p.2.

9   *The Examiner* — 14 January 1843 p.14.

10  *Morning Chronicle* — 30 January 1843 p.2.

11  *Saunders's News-Letter* — 15 May 1843 p.2.

12  *London Evening Standard* — 21 August 1843 p.1.

13  "Colonel" Rufus Welch was an American circus proprietor, who had organised Stone's tour of England and then provided the finance that enabled Hernandez and Stone to establish their own circus.

14  *Ibid.* 5 — 3 April 1852 p.1.

15  *The Era* — 16 May 1852 p.1.

16  *Nottingham Guardian* — 4 November 1852 p.4.

17  Welch became ill in November 1852 and turned his circuses over to his employees.

In America they were run as cooperative enterprises. He died in 1856.

18  *Leeds Times* — 22 January 1853 p.5.

19  James Newsome was born in 1824 in Newcastle-upon-Tyne and was another apprentice of William Batty.

20  *Bath Chronicle and Weekly Gazette* — 18 January 1855 p.3.

21  *Morning Advertiser* — 5 February 1855 p.8. — "To Equestrians, Farmers, and Others. — Sale of valuable Horses, Harness, Waggons, Tents, Vans, light Gigs, American Carriages with Heads, closed Vans, Forty Ring and useful Machine Horses, Ponies and valuable Effects, all in capital condition and good working order, and sold in consequence of a Dissolution of Partnership, being the entire genuine Stock of Messrs. Hernandez, Stone and Newsom, The Great American Equestrian Company. MR. E.T. SMITH is instructed to Dispose of by Public Auction the above valuable PROPERTY, at Mr. Lansley's, the Equestrian Riding School and Circus, Bristol-road, Bath ...". — E.T. Smith himself was to purchase many of the assets and rename the circus, "E.T. Smith's Leviathan Equestrian Company". Eaton Stone was retained as manager, while Hernandez and Newcome formed another circus company.

22  Edward Tyrell Smith was an inveterate speculator. The son of an Admiral, he followed a number of careers — policeman, publican, restaurateur and, at one time, proprietor of the Sunday Times. His greatest success was in theatre management.

23  *The Theatre Royal: Management*, in Survey of London: Volume 35, the Theatre Royal, Drury Lane, and the Royal Opera House, Covent Garden, ed. Sheppard, F.H.W (1970), pp. 9-29. British History Online http://www.british-history.ac.uk/survey-london/vol35/pp9-29, accessed 16 August 2016.

24  *Worcester Journal* — 30 December 1854 p.5. — THE CIRCUS. — This favourite place of amusement closed last week, under circumstances of a peculiarly unpleasant nature. The proprietor, M. Pablo Fanque, who turns out to be Mr. Wm. Darby, formerly an apprentice to Mr. Batty, had, it seems, become involved in pecuniary engagements with that well-known equestrian, to whom he had given a bill of sale upon the whole of the "properties" of the establishment. Execution had been taken under its provisions, and as all attempts to arrange matters amicably have failed, Mr. Higgs offers the whole stud, &c., for auction tomorrow (Saturday).

25  " ... money was paid by Pablo on account till 1854. Mr. Bullard's debt was reduced to £50, and Mr. Batty's to £308 14s. 10d. The defendant [Batty] then paid off Mr. Bullard and took security for the two sums, leaving the house, &c, in Pablo's possession, at a rent £20 a week, and to pay all expenses, and ultimately it was reduced to £10 a week." — *Norfolk Chronicle* — 2 July 1859 p.3.

26  *Ibid.* 7 — 28 February 1855 p.4.

27  There were a number of factors that set these American circuses apart from their British rivals over the next few decades: the use of tents rather than semi-permanent buildings, the construction of highly ornate circus wagons, transportation by rail and the multiplication of circus rings from one to three. J. Purdy Brown of Delaware was the first American circus proprietor to take his circus on the road with a tent in 1825.

28  *Ibid.* 7 — 25 April 1857 p.1.

29  *Birmingham Daily Post* — 16 April 1858 p.1.

30  *Bolton Chronicle* — 25 September 1858 p.6. — "SEIZURE OF PABLO FANQUE'S

CIRCUS FOR DEBT ... the performers ... were at the time under a dark cloud of adversity, their stud, and all things belonging to them, being seized under a bill of sale, for debts contracted in another locality; and the company, consisting of parents and children, were once turned adrift, houseless and homeless, to seek fortunes as they could."

31  *Bradford Observer* — 14 October 1858 p.5.
32  *Ibid.* 18 — 6 November 1858 p.4.
33  *Ibid.* 30 — 16 December 1858 p.8.
34  *Birmingham Journal* — 18 December 1858 p.7.
35  *Leeds Intelligencer* — 5 February 1859 p.7.
36  *Ibid.*
37  *Ibid.* 15 — 6 February 1859 p.10.
38  *Liverpool Mercury* — 15 January 1859 p.1. — "FOR SIX NIGHTS ONLY, ROYAL COLOSSEUM, /PARADISE-STREET / IMMENSE SUCCESS, / Re-engagement of / PABLO FANQUE AND THE BLACK MARE BEDA, THE WONDER OF THE WORLD."
39  *Glasgow Herald* — 5 March 1859 p.1. — "MACARTE & CLARKE'S MAGIC RING, Glasgow Green. / On MONDAY, MARCH 7, and during the Week, the Renowned / PABLO FANQUE / Will have the honour of making his appearance with his Celebrated Mare / BEDA / Universally acknowledged the most perfectly-trained Horse in the World."
40  *Bell's Life in London and Sporting Chronicle* — 27 March 1859 p.1. — "BY ORDER of the COURT of BANKRUPTCY for the LEEDS DISTRICT. — To Circus Proprietors, Equestrians, and Others. — Important Sale. — TO be SOLD by AUCTION, by Mr G. D. MOXON, at the house of Mr John T. Sweeting, the Great Bull Inn, in Wakefield, in the county York, on Thursday, March 31st at 3 o'clock in the afternoon precisely unless previously disposed of by private contract, of which due notice will given, the celebrated black mare BEDA, late the property of William Darby, commonly known "Pablo Fanque," travelling comedian, circus proprietor, and dealer in horses, and bankrupt. The performances of the mare "Beda" are so well known to circus proprietors and managers, and the public generally, and so highly appreciated that any attempt to expatiate upon her value, within the compass of an advertisement, would be superfluous. Permission to view the mare, by ticket, may be obtained on application to B. Foster, carrier, Wakefield, and further particulars are available on applying to the auctioneer, at his offices in Wakefield and Pontefract."
41  James (Jem) Myers, an equestrian and circus owner, had sold a tent for £100 13s, and placards for a further £100, to Pablo in March 1858.
42  *Ibid.* 18 — 4 June 1859 p.3.
43  The official assignee in a bankruptcy case is the person who administers and receives the bankrupt's estate. Batty had seized the goods as the main creditor, failing to take into account the rights of other potential creditors. If it could be established that he was de facto the official assignee, he would be legally responsible for distributing the assets fairly among the creditors. Batty was to argue he was the owner of the goods and as such they were not part of William Darby's estate.
44  *Ibid.* 12 — 25 June 1859 p.7.
45  Wallett, W. F. (1884) *The Public Life of W. F. Wallett, the Queen's Jester: An*

*Autobiography of Forty Years Professional Experience & Travels in the United Kingdom, The United States of America (including California), Canada, South America, Mexico and the West Indies.* p.117 – 119.

46  *Ibid.* 15 – 19 December 1858 p.9. – "Mr. Wallett, the Clown, offered proofs for £113, which was denied by Darbey [sic], who asserted that he had paid Wallett every shilling he owed him. It was attempted to prove that a partnership had existed between Darbey [sic] and Wallett, but failed. The learned Commissioner remarked that it was not of much consequence whether the disputed claim was allowed or not, as there was only £149 assets to pay £2,800 debts, and that there would consequently be nothing to pay any creditor."

47  *Ibid.* 2 – 29 March 1860 p.2. – "DISCHARGED BANKRUPTS. – William Darby, otherwise known by the name of Pablo Fanque, equestrian and dealer in horses, and residing in Glasgow, was sequestrated on 7th February, 1860, and discharged on 27th March, 1860, on composition of 6d. per pound."

48  *Ibid.* 2 – 18 February 1860 p.2. – "PABLO FANQUE'S CIRCUS. – Last night, Mr. Pablo Fanque, the successful horse trainer, exhibited for the first time a beautiful chestnut mare, named 'Lady Ayr', in his circus on the Green. Many of our readers will remember the celebrated mare, 'Beda,' which under Mr. Fanque's training, became one of the best performing animals ever seen. But that valuable mare being now dead, Mr. Fanque set about training another; from her performances last night it was palpable that her owner has made another decided hit. Although, as we are informed, 'Lady Ayr' had only been under training for three weeks, she went through the most astonishing performances with great ease. Pablo was loudly applauded by the auditory for his success."

49  *Ibid.* 15 – 15 January 1860 p.1. – "Just published, price One Shilling, HORSE TRAINING and HORSE TAMING: OR, THE RAREY SHOWMAN SHOWN UP, A Practical Treatise on the Horse, with simple Instructions how to subdue, treat, and teach him; how to know his age correctly; with cures for coughs, colds, strains, sprains, splints, spavils, curbs, capt hacks, swelled legs, facy, rheumatism; also methods for relieving broken-winded horses, &c. By PABLO FANQUE,
Late Proprietor of the Principal Provincial Royal Amphitheatres and Circuses in England, Ireland, and Scotland. With numerous Illustrations.
Agents wanted for the sale of the above Publication. A liberal allowance will be made. Parties desirous of becoming Agents would do well to send for one Copy to WILLIAM GILCHRIST, Steam Power Printer, 182, Trongate, Glasgow. On receipt of Twelve Postage Stamps, A Copy will be sent, post free, for approval. A printed form, with the percentage allowed, will be sent with each Copy ordered."

50  *Blackburn Standard* – 13 June 1860 p.3.

51  *Burnley Advertiser* – 14 July 1860 p.3.

52  *Ibid.* 31 – 2 August 1860 p.1.

53  *Ibid.* 15 – 20 November 1859 p.6.

54  *Birmingham Mail* – 6 May 1871 p.4.

55  *Yorkshire Post and Leeds Intelligencer* – 6 May 1871 p.5.

56  Many examples of his popularity in local newspapers can be found. The trade

paper remarked, "BRADFORD / CIRCUS. — Mr Pablo Fanque pitched his tent in this town on Wednesday week, and has since enjoyed a good run of business. Mr. Fanque is very popular here, as he has the reputation of always providing an entertainment worthy of patronage. This visit he has not disappointed the expectations of his numerous patrons, as he is accompanied by a clever troupe of equestrians, acrobats, &c., incidental to this class of entertainment." — *Ibid.* 15 — 12 August 1860 p.11.

57  The Lancashire Cotton Famine (1861–65) was a depression in the cotton manufacturing districts of the north-west. It was first brought about by overproduction at a time of contracting world markets, but was then extended by a blockade of southern state ports by the north during the American Civil War. This created a shortage of suitable raw material coming into Britain.

58  *Ibid.* 18 — 12 July 1862 p.5.

59  *Newcastle Daily Chronicle* — 18 April 1863 — "The Alhambra Circus. — Thursday night, the Tyne Concert Hall re-opened under the above designation with a highly talented equestrian troupe, directed by Mr. Pablo Fanque. During the recess the building has been renovated and newly decorated, and a marvellous metamorphosis has been effected in its interior aspect. Built originally for a circus, the spacious ring has been restored, and is, probably, not inferior in dimensions to that of any similar establishment in the kingdom. The boxes are commodious and comfortably fitted with stuffed seats and chairs. The pit and gallery have been considerably enlarged, and from all parts of the building unobstructed view of the performances may be obtained. The columns which support the roof have been painted a delicate shade green, also the facade of promenade and gallery, which produces a most airy and agreeable effect. A new and massive iron chandelier diffuses a brilliant light over the arena. ... We congratulate Mr. Stanley on his first successful venture in the circus line of amusement, and the really admirable manner in which, aided by the indefatigable exertions of Mr. Kinnear, Mr. Pablo Fanque's agent, he has adapted the building for equestrian purposes."

60  *Penny Despatch and Irish Weekly Newspaper* — December 1866 p.5.

61  *Ibid.* 15 — 10 February 1867 p.12.

62  *Ibid.* 15 — 10 September 1865 p.1. — "Notice to Equestrian Managers and others, PABLO FANQUE and his Three Talented Pupils, with Three Ring Horses and one Trick Horse, or can come with Two Ring and a Trick Horse, will be at Liberty after Saturday, Sept. 16th, for short engagements. Direct, Waddington's Circus, Haslingden, Sept. 18th and 19th; Rautonstall, 20th and 21st; Waterpost, 22d and 23d."

63  *Ibid.* 15 — 31 December 1865 p.16. — PARENTS and GUARDIANS in the Equestrian Profession. — "Mr. PABLO FANQUE would be happy to arrange with the Above for a little Boy and Girl; those who have had some little Experience in the Business preferred, as it would be a good opportunity for those who wish to be made perfect in the Equestrian Profession. For length of time and full particulars, address, Mr. PABLO FANQUE, Pinders' Circus, South Shields."

64  *Ibid.* 15 — 5 March 1881 p.3.

65  *Huddersfield Chronicle* — 13 May 1871 p.8.

# 6

# A Romance of Real Life

*His history was really a romance of real life. A splendid rider, fearless and enterprising in spirit, nothing daunted him, not even the dark clouds of adversity; and to listen to his stories of equestrian experience, and thus be brought vividly, almost face to face, with the great people who patronised him and his establishment, was like reading the story of a Paladin or a Crusader of old. The writer of this notice has often requested Pablo to furnish him with the most salient and racy incidents of his career, but the day was put off until the angel of death stepped in, and finally closed the arrangement.*

Leeds Times – 6 May 1871

Within the lifetime of William Darby (1810 – 1871), Britain underwent significant social and economic change. Rapid industrialisation and the transport revolution fuelled substantial growth in population centred on the expanding towns of the north of England.  The working people of these industrial towns had more money than previous generations to spend on leisure. They, together with a middle class, who sought both excitement and moral propriety based in family-orientated entertainment, provided a ready audience for a growing leisure industry. The circus fulfilled a specific function. Its raison d'être was to allow the audience to enter another world, in which the realities of life were temporarily suspended. Rooted in pre-industrial forms of entertainment performed by itinerant players on feast days and the village green, the circus contrasted the rigours of life in the industrial towns by providing a longing for the simplicity of the past.

In 1854, Charles Dickens published *Hard Times*, firstly in serial format', then as a completed work. Dickens' favourable portrayal of the circus became his metaphor for the importance of 'fancy' or imagination in life, in contrast to blind and uncaring utilitarianism that reduced individuals to numbers and society to 'facts'[2]. Dickens' work undoubtedly influenced cultural perceptions of the circus at the time and sets the background for understanding the nostalgia that manifested itself so readily in Fanque's circus in the late 1860s. Local newspapers reflect the view that the coming of Pablo's circus was not just an annual tradition, but also a harking back to a past that had been somehow lost[3]. Fanque himself exploited this in his advertising:

**PABLO FANQUE'S CIRCUS**
Mr. PABLO FANQUE, Director of the Circus Troupe now performing in the Orchard, begs to remind his friends and patrons that his performances are in every respect equal to those of "by-gone days," when his Company and great Troupe of Horses joined in the Procession of the Guild of 1842.
Mr. Pablo Fanque again wishes to impress on the minds of the Prestonians that it is now twenty-six years — when but a young man — he came amongst them, "when in the fresh prime of life, and bloom of prosperity." From that day to this, either in sunshine or darkness, his heart has been amongst those who cherished and supported him.
Grant it in the present day, bubble and froth, empty air with gilded outside show and meagre inside, seem to take the ignorant by storm. Give but one look to Pablo's Circus you are then bound to visit again and again; it will remind you of the days when you were children when you went with your pa's and ma's to see Pablo and his noble and educated steed, "Beda," whose instinct and docility has been the theme and admiration of thronging and delighted audiences.[4]

While the circus had always promised colour, by the 1860s many of Fanque's rivals had integrated other more exotic forms of entertainment, such as wild beasts, into their shows. Such a trend had been initiated as long ago as the 1830s by Ducrow[5] and Batty[6], but in the first half of the century they were mostly the preserve of menageries, such as that owned by Wombwell, and found alongside other booths at the annual fairs. Wombwell's menagerie showed a range of exotic animals:

WILD BEASTS. — It will be observed, from an advertisement in another column, that Wombwell's royal menagerie is still exhibiting in the fair. We have paid a visit to the exhibition, and after witnessing the control exercised by the keepers, over the most ferocious animals of the brute creation, were highly gratified with a sight of the giraffe, or camel-leopard, an animal never seen here before, but in Van Amburgh's collection. It is a tall and handsome quadruped, imported from the interior of Abyssinia, in Africa, and we are informed, was purchased by Mr. Wombwell, at a cost of £1,500. The scholars of the Lancasterian schools were yesterday gratuitously admitted, by Mr. Wombwell, to see the exhibition.[7]

Menageries also involved human performance with animals. Inevitably this was highly dangerous, as Ellen Bright, a seventeen year

*Ellen Bright, the seventeen year old "Lion Queen" was attacked by a tiger and died of her injuries at Chatham, 1850.*

old performer, found to her cost in January 1850 while Wombwell's was at Chatham:

> On Saturday evening last, an inquest was held at the Golden Lion Inn, Chatham, before J. Hind, Esq., coroner for West Kent, touching the death of Ellen Bright, a young girl, aged 17 years, who was killed the previous evening by a tiger, in the establishment of Mr. George Wombwell, which had arrived in that town for exhibition on the preceding day. The deceased, who was denominated, 'the Lion Queen,' had the honour of performing before her Majesty some time since, at Windsor Castle; and as will be seen from the evidence, was going through the usual evolutions with a lion and tiger at the time she met with her melancholy death. [8]

These menageries were the forerunners of performance with exotic animals that became a mainstay of the American travelling circus in Britain. However, while menageries continued to exist at fairs and other traditional gatherings well beyond the end of the century, there was little point in smaller circuses, such as Pablo's, providing this type of entertainment. It was enough to provide traditional circus fare and occupy a niche that larger establishments had forsaken.

*Jem Mace, from Beeston, Norfolk, was first to be recognised as a world boxing champion.*

Although not exploiting the exotic, Fanque did however follow other trends popular at the time to bring in the crowds. For example, in May 1863, while at the Tyne Concert Hall in Newcastle, he introduced the audience to Robert Chambers[9], the champion professional sculler, and presented him with a silver cup to recognise his achievement.[10] Pablo's biggest attraction was Jem Mace[11], later to be recognised as the bare-knuckle boxing Champion of World, who gave exhibition matches for him from August to October 1861.[12]

The appeal of Pablo Fanque's circus during the 1860s was that it tapped into important cultural norms for the period. Nostalgia for an idyllic rural past had to be balanced with the hard commercial and industrial reality of the time. The fairground, attached to town and city fairs, had long had a reputation for dishonesty and vice, and were considered locations where the social order was threatened by the mingling of classes. To counter this circus proprietors adopted the language and practice of respectability. Fanque presented his establishment as very much part of the community. In addition to regular appearances in the same towns, he emphasised value wherever he went:

> PABLO'S CIRCUS, BOAR-LANE, LEEDS.
> LOOK! LOOK! LOOK !
> RESERVED SEATS, 2s.; BOXES, 1s.; PIT, 6d.; GALLERY, 3d
>
> The CIRCUS lately occupied by Mr. Bell, Boar-lane, Leeds, will be RE-OPENED on Monday, JANUARY 14TH, 1861, under the management of your old favourite PABLO FANQUE, for a short season only. It would be useless to make any long comment upon the merits of the Company that he intends to bring with him; his character is well-known for procuring Talent for the amusement of the Public, and that always at a cheap rate, so that all classes have an opportunity of paying a visit to amuse themselves, and appreciate the performances there introduced, and charged so to keep up the character, the Circus will be Re-Opened on Monday, January 14th, 1861, at the following prices: — Reserved Seats. 2s.; Boxes, Is.; Pit, 6d.; Gallery, 3d.[13]

Mr. Pablo Fanque's Circus Sunderland.— Monday evening, Mr. Pablo Fanque and his talented company of equestrians opened a series of performances at Sunderland, in a commodious and comfortable marquee erected in the field adjoining the Palatine Hotel, Borough Road. There was a good audience, and excellent arrangements connected with the marquee appeared to give general satisfaction. The comfort or convenience of those whose means compel them to pay the lower charge for admission is seldom studied [in the] circus, as they are generally huddled together round the ring, but at Mr. Fanque's establishment every one is accommodated with a comfortable seat.[14]

Another strategy was to provide philanthropic charity, and, given his background, it is perhaps not surprising that he was often generous towards the very poorest in society:

Treat to Workhouse Children. — On Tuesday ı afternoon Mr. Pablo Fanque invited the children resident in the Hull and Sculcoates Workhouses to witness the performance at his Circus, and they attended and were highly delighted with the treat. Oranges, &c., were provided for the children by Messrs. Story and Graves, two of the guardians of the poor for Holy Trinity and St. Mary, and their kindness and that of Mr. Pablo Fanque appeared to be very highly appreciated.[15]

Despite this quest for respectability the circus was met with suspicion in some quarters, being viewed as immoral and likely to corrupt:

## THE ROYAL CIRCUS.
## SURREY QUARTER SESSIONS.

Yesterday came on the business of hearing the applications of the Proprietors of the Royal Circus and Astley's Amphitheatre for a renewal of their Annual Licence, under the provisions of the Statute 25 Geo. II. — Mr. Astley's went over tolerably easy.
To the licencing of the unfortunate Proprietors of the Royal Circus a strong opposition was made by the tender conscienced [sic] Members of the Society for the Suppression of Vice and Immorality, who in urgent terms laboured to shew the dangerous tendency the keeping of such a place had to corrupt the morals of the rising generation. Their description of the conduct of the frequenters was painted in glowing colours, and the interferences they drew were calculated to impress on the Bench, that the house ought not to be licensed.
In reply, on the part of the distressed Applicants, it was argued, that their performances were marked with moral sentiment and loyalty. Some of the Magistrates observed, they had frequently

visited that Theatre with great gratification, and found no greater breach of morality there than at the Opera or the Winter Theatres. Persons at all public Theatres would at times be found to transgress the bounds of decent decorum. Two Police Officers were stationed there every evening to keep as good order as possible, and were successful in doing so ...[16]

The perception that cheap amusements, aimed at the working classes, inevitably produced degenerate behaviour persisted throughout the century despite evidence to the contrary. Civic authorities, attempting to grapple with the social consequences of industrial growth within their towns, debated the effect of commercial entertainment on the working population. At a public meeting in Bradford, called in June 1849, to discuss the "moral condition of the town", the concern felt by the middle class population was mirrored in many of the industrial towns. The mayor, and convenor of the meeting, Titus Salt outlined its purpose:

He has long seen that there was a want of adequate religious instruction and also of the means of innocent recreation for the working classes; and with the advice of a few friends, he has called this meeting to confer together, in order to see what could be done to improve the religious and moral position of the borough.[17]

Alderman Forbes noted that:

... for whilst it might be well to have concerts and similar amusements, he had doubts as to their having the effect of correcting evil, although they might palliate it to a certain extent. He did not approve of the population being brought together for recreations and amusements of that kind late on Saturday evenings. He thought it would be a far better course if the shops and markets were closed earlier, and other measures adopted to convince the population that on Saturday evenings they ought to be directing their attention to the solemn engagements of the Sabbath, for although the utmost care were exercised, there were highly contaminating influences in connexion with the assemblages of the character he has alluded to.[18]

Many at the meeting saw the provision of suitable amusements, such as concerts and the circus, as taking the working population away from beer-houses:

> ... Alderman Smith read a letter from Mr. Beswick of Manchester, who bore testimony to the fact that, whenever a concert occurred on a large scale, where the working people were admitted at a cheap rate, the beer-houses and other low places, where music, dancing and other amusements took place, were deserted. He believed that the beer-house as at present conducted was fraught with evil; ... since Wallett's circus had been open, many of the beer houses in the town had been deserted.[19]

Circus proprietors also sought to reassure their potential audience of the propriety of their performance and its effect on those watching:

> Mons. PABLO FANQUE thinks it may be necessary to offer an explanation relative to the effect and moral import of each performance. Innocent recreation has, by the rigid professors of morality and discipline, been considered an effective spur to the youthful mind, when judiciously employed moments of relaxation from the graver intricacies of the arts and sciences, or rather branches of complicated education. From the ordinary occupation of life, to unmbend [sic] the attention to light subjects of amusement may give zeal that can increase application and be more profitable than the solitary pleasures of seclusion, or the more open dissipations of life. Public amusements are but too often conducted in a manner regardless of the morals of the visiters [sic], and thereby many persons of particular sects, or moral characters, entirely absent themselves from theatres of public representations. To obviate such objections, it is the present intention to produce a series of Olympic exploits, at once astonishing and recreative, and, so cautious will be the selection, that the tender father, the affectionate husband, or admiring lover, need not fear the blush of modesty will ever be excited by an exhibition within the arena. Dublin, Cork, Limerick, Liverpool, Manchester, and Brighton the company has been honoured with the highest approbation from eminent divines of all sects, and the support of many persons who never practice visiting public exhibitions.[20]

But there was also determined opposition that often verged on intimidation:

> On Monday last, Mon. Pablo Fanque Darby's performing company in horsemanship visited Grantham. In the evening the tent was crowded to the ceiling, notwithstanding a bigoted attempt to frighten juveniles and antiquated ladies from attending. One of the performers stated that he thought this the only town in which an individual could be found who considered it offensive in the eyes of the Almighty to witness the agility of men and the docility of horses.[21]

While some concentrated on the effect circus entertainment had on the wider population, others applied evangelical morality to the performers themselves, and in particular, women and children.

In December 1860, Fanque's circus was visiting Chadwick's Orchard once again in Preston. Madame Salvi was to perform her high wire act outside, presumably to promote the performance that evening.

> PABLO FANQUE'S CIRCUS. — EXCITING AND FRIGHTFUL SCENE — The performances in this circus ... are sustained with great ability. The equestrianism, "tumbling," tight-rope dancing &c. are in many respects excellent, and meet, as their reward, with a deal of public support. On Wednesday, however, a mishap occurred to one of the artistes which produced a good deal of sensation in the town, and which might very easily have been attended with serious consequences. It was announced that Madame Salvi would walk along a thin twisted wire cable, stretching from the top of the circus (outside) to a block fixed a little above the front entrance to the establishment. Two o'clock was the hour specified for this feat, and by that time a very large number of persons had congregated in the Orchard to witness its accomplishment. Some persons thought that this daring performance would never be carried into effect, the altitude of the wire being so great, whilst others, seeing the wire had been duly fixed, felt confident that there was no mistake about the matter. A little after two o'clock Madame Salvi made her appearance, and immediately afterwards ascended a ladder in front of the wire. A great deal of anxiety was now

manifested. At length she started, and progressed very steadily until within ten or twelve yards of the end, when, to the alarm of all present, and the screams of some, one of the ropes which held the wire to the top of the circus gave way. This accident completely destroyed the equilibrium of Madame Salvi, and she was thrown off the wire. In descending, however, she managed to catch the wire with one of her arms, and remained suspended in this frightful position for about half a minute, after which she secured the wire with her hands, her body swinging in the air full length. In a short time a number of men got a ladder, and reared it to the roof of the circus. Madame Salvi, who was hanging immediately above them, managed, after some little difficulty, to find the ladder with her feet. She then descended amid the cheers of the anxious crowd, and eventually landed safety upon the ground. The feat was not attempted again.[22]

Despite this lucky escape, Madame Salvi was to repeat the outdoor performance the following March:

SCARBOROUGH

NARROW ESCAPE, — Madame Salvi, a daring wire-walker attached to the establishment of Mons. Pablo Fanque, at present at Rock Gardens, Scarborough, had a narrow escape for her life, or at least her limbs, on Saturday afternoon last. She announced to ascend a wire-rope from the gardens to the top of the saloon, — a feat which she accomplished very cleverly. In returning, however, and while performing some movements on the rope, the wind, which had blown in gusts during the afternoon, caused her to lose her balance, and she slipped off the wire, to the great consternation of the beholders. With remarkable presence of mind, she seized the wire with her hands, and hung on for several minutes, calling loudly for help. At length, as soon as possible, the wire was slackened, and Madame Salvi was drawn to the side of the bank, and released from her critical position. Had she fallen to the ground she could not have escaped serious injury. The screams of many in the crowd were louder than the cries of Madame Salvi herself.[23]

Regardless of these experiences, in 1862, Madame Salvi was to fall for a third time on returning to Chadwick's Orchard in Preston[24].

The pressure to perform more dangerous and daring acts had been precipitated by the arrival in Britain of Blondin, the French high-wire walker, in 1861. He had gained his reputation in America in the late 1850s and his fortune had been secured when he crossed the Niagara gorge on 30 June 1859. He was to do this a number of times, always in more daring ways — blindfold, in a sack, or carrying a man on his back.

While such incidents illustrated the precarious and dangerous nature of performance in the circus, the reason why individuals chose to put themselves at peril, or why such performances attracted large audiences, drew little comment from the general public. The aura of the circus was so strong that few questioned, except on religious grounds, the social and ethical reasons for circus performance. Attitudes were to change though in July 1863, when Selina Powell was to fall to her death in front of thousands of spectators at Aston Park, Birmingham.

Selina Powell, one of the many female wire-walkers to call themselves the female or Madame "Blondin", adopted similar encumbrances to add thrills to her performances:

> ... at a quarter past five the programme announced in large letters that "Madame Geneive, the Female Blondin, the only real and legitimate performer of Blondin's great feats, walking the rope shackled in chains, feet in baskets, blindfolded, enveloped in a sack, &c."[25]

Her performance was delayed due to a breeze and she did not mount the ladder until later:

> At about half-past six o'clock Madame Geneive ascended the ladder, and taking the balance-pole in her hands, stepped out on the rope with much confidence. She walked half way across the rope, and then returning she had two very heavy chains tied to her hands and feet. Her action was not impeded: for the right foot tied to the right hand and the left foot to the left hand, the chains being sufficiently long to allow her to make free use of hands and feet. The chains encumbered her only by their weight. Again she walked along the rope without the slightest apparent trepidation.

She walked the whole length of the rope stepping over the point of the upright pole by which the rope was supported in the centre. At the other end of the rope she received from a man, who was in attendance, a bag or sack, which she placed over her head and shoulders. Again she went upon the rope, stepping with confidence, but had only gone about a yard when there was a crash, and before the cry of horror had died from

*Punch's cartoon illustrating the death of Selina Powell at Aston Park in July 1863.*

the lips of the spectators, Madame Geneive had fallen at the feet of her husband and was dead. The crowd rushed towards the spot, but the police were able to keep a small space around the dead woman.[26]

Selina Powell's death might have attracted no more attention than the death of other circus performers at the time had it not been discovered, on examination by a doctor at the scene, that she was between six and eight months pregnant. Further investigation by the Birmingham Daily Post revealed the circumstances of the family:

We have ascertained that the real name of this "Female Blondin" is Powell and that she is a native of our town. Some years ago her husband had his ribs broken by accident, rendering him incapable of work, and since that time the maintenance of himself and a family of some six or seven children - we have not been able to ascertain the precise number - has rested with his wife. Her earnings as a rope dancer have been small and precarious, and, as a consequence the family have been in a state of great poverty. The Foresters[27] making her an advantageous offer, she, notwithstanding her delicate state of health, consented to go through her dangerous feats for the amusement of the sensation loving people of Birmingham, with the disastrous result known to our readers and thus the melancholy of this affair is heightened by the fact that in addition to the two deaths involved - that of the mother and her child unborn - a large family of young children and an invalid father are left unprovided for.[28]

The death at Aston Park awakened Victorian concerns over the nature and role of women, death, the family and childhood, and threw a spotlight on circus performance, artistic regulation and the commercialisation of leisure. The incident drew comment from Queen Victoria herself, despite having patronised the circus in earlier decades, permitting command performances in Brighton at the Pavilion. In a letter to the Mayor of Birmingham, her representative wrote:

> Sir — The Queen has commanded me to express to you the pain with which her Majesty has read the account of a fatal accident which has occurred during a fête at Aston Park, Birmingham.
>
> Her Majesty cannot refrain from making it known through you her personal feelings of horror that one of her subjects — a female — should have been sacrificed to the gratification of the demoralising taste, unfortunately prevalent, for exhibitions attended with the greatest danger to the performers.
>
> Were proof wanting that such exhibitions are demoralising, I am commanded to remark that it would be at once found in the decision arrived at during the festivities, the hilarity, and the sports of the occasion after an event so melancholy.
>
> The Queen trusts that you, in common with the rest of the people of Birmingham, will use your influence to prevent in future the degradation of such exhibitions of the park which was gladly opened by her Majesty and the beloved Prince Consort, in the hope that it would be made serviceable for the healthy exercise and rational recreation of the people.[29]

Despite the Queen's comments, which resonated with many in Victorian society, the public's desire to see dangerous performances did not diminish. The performance of females was controversial, not only because of the danger involved, but also the likelihood of affronting Victorian attitudes towards sex and social cohesion. This led to some denouncing performance as a form of cruelty, not only to women and children, but also to society itself:

## FEMALE ACROBATS

The cruelty of our public exhibitions is not a novel subject, a sort of intermittent protest being made on the topic whenever an accident, as it is termed occurs. Within the last twelvemonth, however, a fashion of amusement has set in in this way that deserves mention, especially at the present season. We refer to the employment of women and children, or rather infants, as acrobats.

It will be remembered that some years ago Her Majesty expressed herself in sufficiently emphatic terms against the encouragement given to displays of the female somnambulist; since then however, so far from the business being abandoned or mitigated, it has been taken up with increasing vigour and enterprise, until the most daring feats of male tumblers are matched and rivalled by gymnasts of the other sex. The music-halls are the favourite patrons of these unhappy artists. In these haunts the comic song, the nigger dance, and the ballet, serve to lead up to the great sensation of the evening, when a woman, clothed in a dress far more unwomanly than rags, is swung upon ropes and jerked between strings of the trapeze over the heads of an audience who are pleasantly excited over the chance of the poor creature breaking her neck before the performance concluded. Now and again the papers would record the fall of a lady Leotard, and her retirement into cripplehood from her profession. These narratives gave zest to the spectacles. ... We do not so much care to dwell upon the impropriety of this female acrobatism as upon its cruelty. It becoming competitive in boldness and risk. These sorry sights are training the people who look on them into a taste for the most vicious of all pleasures, the pleasure of wanton excitement provoked by the prospect of seeing a woman do violence to every instinct of her nature — risk her life and limbs upon a skill that has been acquired at a terrible cost and sacrifice.[30]

While moral indignation was concerned with women performers parliamentary debates in the 1860s and 70s centred on the wider issue of child performers. Legislation regarding child labour had been enacted to curb the worst abuses in factories and mines in the 1830s and 1840s, but those involved in the entertainment industries remained untouched. Given the very visible nature of children, whether performing in the ring or at fairs and festivals, it was only a matter of time that concern led to action. The vast majority of child prodigies were the offspring of performers, brought up in the trade, but some, as we have seen, were apprenticed to showmen such as Fanque, either because their parents saw it as a way to provide for them, or the child had a penchant for circus performance. One of these was John Henry Walker, the famous clown called "Whimsical" Walker, who was one of many who owed their eventual success to Pablo Fanque. In his autobiography[31], Walker describes how

THEATRE ROYAL, DRURY LANE, LONDON.
Pantomime 1913–14.–15–16–17–18–19
1920 & 1921.

Faithfully yours, Whimsical Walker.

*Whimsical Walker in the 1920s.*

his father was a manager with Cooke's Circus, and following the death of his first wife gave up the circus life on marrying again. Walker, at the age of eight, ran away from home joining a tumbling booth at Knott Mill Fair. Having been caught and brought home, his waywardness led to his father sending him to Pablo. Walker's reminiscences of his apprenticeship shows the high regard he felt for William Darby and provides some insight into the way in which Fanque treated and trained his apprentices during the late 1860s:

Pablo Fangue [sic], a coloured gentleman, was a thorough master of his profession, and I have to thank him for what I subsequently became without vanity may I say it? — the greatest celebrity in my particular line in the circus business. He taught me to ride, to tumble, to perform on the trapeze, to vault over horses, and indeed all the intricacies belonging to circus life. I must admit that I was not over good at riding — you see, my face was not too beautiful — so I was made a clown. I confess that I like clowning, as the audience often threw oranges and money into the ring when I made them laugh, as I often did.

Training for the circus meant much harder work than people may imagine. There were three boy apprentices besides myself, and a girl (Fanny Bluring). We boys had to get up at 6 o'clock every morning to look after the horses, breakfast was at 8, practice at 8.30, and school at 9, excepting when we were performing at fairs. Pablo Fangue did his duty towards us very conscientiously and sent us to church on Sunday mornings. Of course, we preferred playing marbles, and to satisfy our master, who always asked us what the text was, we used to learn one by heart beforehand. Maybe the good words came too trippingly off our tongues and so excited his suspicions, and he caught us out by going unseen by us to the same church. That day at dinner he was unusually nice and said quite amicably, "Well, my boys, have you all been to church?" "Yes, sir," we chanted." "And was it a nice sermon?" "Oh, yes, sir." "And what were the words?" "Jesus wept." "Ah, and all of you will too" —and we did.

He certainly knew something about boys' ways, did Pablo Fangue. We used to have sundry threepenny and fourpenny pieces given to us during the week, and clever little Fanny Bluring was our banker. All she had to do was to drop the little coins down the bag-like receptacle for the flat piece of wood in front of her old-fashioned stays, and there they remained in safety till we wanted them on Sunday, when we would gorge ourselves with ice creams, nuts, gingerbread, and anything we fancied. In Glasgow we spent no end of shillings with an ice cream merchant in the Saltmarket, and our master suspecting the reason why we couldn't eat any dinner conspired with the iceman. The next time we had ice creams —

but I draw a veil over the sequel. For months after I could never face an ice cream.

I was with Pablo until he died. I was then fourteen and I fancy I knew more about animals than most boys of my age. I was entrusted to buy the hay for the horses; I acted as veterinary surgeon, I could tell when a horse was lame, when he was ill I knew what was the matter with him; and all this useful knowledge I must say I owe to Pablo Fanque. He was certainly one of the best of masters.[32]

Fanque's treatment of apprentices was clearly rigorous when preparing them for the harsh life of being a circus performer. Some did not like it and there are many incidents of his apprentices absconding. For example, Hugh O'Donnell was to run away twice, in 1845[33] and 1846[34]. Circus proprietors were quick to defend themselves against accusations of cruelty with regard to their apprentices. A case in point is the absconding of Joseph Gee, aged fourteen, his sister Jane, aged twelve, and Charles Bradbury, aged ten, from J.H. Emidy's circus in Ireland in 1852. Emidy went to the length of publishing a letter in the Era following an accusation by their fathers that they had not been properly indentured and had been treated cruelly. His response to these accusations highlights both the unconventional nature of circus apprenticeships and the attitude of circus proprietors that may have heightened public anxiety later in the century:

> The entire affair is very easily solved; when it is known that, so soon as they were in a position and had gained a name (through my exertions) in my establishment, it was found more conducive to the benefit of their parents to remove TWO of them clandestinely to London, where an engagement had been secured them without giving me the least notice; and on my subsequently finding this move had taken place, I insisted on the youngest child, who was not so far advanced in its tuition (and despite my asserted cruelty would have been left with me), being removed also with the other two. Mr. Jee asserts they were never apprenticed to me, and challenges me to produce any indenture or binding agreement. According to technicalities, there was no indenture, but there was a written agreement between him and me, such as is usual in our

profession, and which agreement the elder boy, Joseph, removed
with another document which he also considered might be binding
on him — for his own especial purpose, no doubt. With regard to
Mr. Jee, he is perfectly sensible that in forwarding the future welfare
of his children in the profession, I have only exercised that control
and tuition over them which 'becomes a man' towards children
anxious, for their own as well as his interest, as their master in the
absence of their parents.

With reference to Mr. Bradbury's complaint, I have merely to say,
that the cause of injury to his son was through his presenting
himself on one occasion, when a rush took place at the opening of
the circus, at the pay box at which Mrs. Emidy was taking money,
and on which occasion the box was broken down and she narrowly
escaped injury; unfortunately he had his ribs hurt then, but prompt
medical aid was procured by me for him, and the 'lacerated knee
and dreadful black eye' were the result of his falling from his horses
whilst going through his performance carelessly in the circus. It
is too bad to heap these accidents upon me, under the head of
my cruelty, when I had every surgical and medical aid called in to
relieve the sufferer; and as to Mr. Bradbury's assertion as to his
son not being my apprentice I have only to reiterate my former
remark, and that I at present hold his written consent, signed in the
presence of witnesses in the month of February, 1849, and could, if
necessary, appeal to the members of my company, and, though last
not least, to Mons. Tournaire, Pablo Fanque, and Messrs. Thomas
and James Cooke, to testify to my general treatment of these as
well as other children intrusted [sic] to my guardianship. Hoping
you will, with your usual frankness and kindness, give insertion
to this, and excuse the length of my trespassing on your columns
in vindication of my outraged feelings, I am, sir, your obedient
servant, J.H. Emidy Drogheda, Sept. 27th, 1852.[35]

Moral opinion over the treatment of child performers was articulated
by the "waif story," a term used by Anna Davin[36] to describe a strand of
writing that appeared between the mid-1860s and the early 1890s. Circus
apprentices and children provided the perfect subject for many of these
books, given that the author could easily draw on the seductive power of

a circus life as "liberator" from the perceived harshness of a respectable home. Typical of this genre is the book, *A Peep behind the Scenes*, written by Mrs. O.F. Walton[37] and published by the Religious Tract Society in 1877. The main character is Rosalie, the twelve year old daughter of a theatrical booth owner who meets stereotypical characters from the fairground and circus communities. The moral purpose, as suggested by the title, is to warn its readers not to be seduced by the seeming glamour and allure of the circus:

> There were many young girls there, some of them servants in respectable families, where they enjoyed every comfort; yet they looked up at little Rosalie with eyes of admiration and envy. They thought her life was much happier than theirs, and that her lot was greatly to be desired. They looked at the white dress and the pink roses, and contrasted them with their own warm but homely garments; they watched the pretty girl going through her part gracefully and easily, and they contrasted her work with theirs. How interesting, how delightful, they thought, to be doing this, instead of scrubbing floors, or washing clothes, or nursing children!
> But they knew nothing of the life behind the scenes, of the sick mother, the wretched home, the poor and insufficient food, the dirty, ragged frock. They knew nothing of the bitter tears which had just been wiped away, nor of the weary aching of the little feet which were dancing so lightly over the stage.[38]

Walton's book became a best seller and quickly sold more than 2.5 million copies. In 1879 Parliament passed the Children's Dangerous Performances Act being specifically aimed at circuses, music halls and "other places of public amusement". It fined any parent or guardian who caused children under the age of fourteen to take part in any exhibition or performance dangerous to life or limb.

1    *Hard Times* was published in twenty weekly parts in Household Words between 1 April and 12 August 1854.

2    Utilitarianism was the leading social theory of the period and was based on the philosophy of Jeremy Bentham. He argued that human nature was motivated by self-interest, or, more exactly, the balance between pleasure and pain. The principle of utility was that every action was governed by the 'pursuit of happiness'. Bentham developed a method of calculating the value of pleasures and pains, and

one of these measures was the extent or the number of people affected by an action. Hence, "The business of government is to promote the happiness of the society, by punishing and rewarding ... In proportion as an act tends to disturb that happiness, in proportion as the tendency of it is pernicious, will be the demand it creates for punishment."

3   *Rochdale Observer* — 2 May 1868 p.5. — "Pablo Fanque's Circus. — Pablo! Who has not heard of Pablo? How many happy-spent evenings are recalled to memory by the sound of his familiar name. And he is now with us once again ..."

4   *Preston Herald* — 29 February 1868 p.5.

5   *Morning Advertiser* — 11 October 1838 — "ASTLEYS ROYAL AMPHITHEATRE. THIS EVENING Thursday, Oct. 1, the third appearance of the three French and Italian Artistes, Signor Cincelli, Mad. Cincalli, and Mona. Letort. Mr. Van Amburgh will exhibit some new performances with the LIVING LIONS, TIGERS, LEOPARDS, &c. Mr. Ducrow will appear in several new and classical introductions— THE POOR IDIOT; or, The Souterain of Heidelberg. The Idiot, Mr. Ducrow. The Four Seasons by La Petite Louise Ducrow; new Act by Master Adams the Young Clown; Arab Feats Messrs. Jackson, Fraser, and Daly. Mr. Ducrow will also perform with his Infant Prodigy and other Pupils, THE MAGIC BELL AND THE ENCHANTED FLUTE; or The Toad In Hole. The Cavalcade of All Nations. To conclude with PAT'S VAGARIES."

6   William Batty ran his own menagerie as an adjunct to his travelling circus from 1839 to 1842. He sold it to Wombwell in January 1842, following his decision to stop travelling when he took over Astley's.

7   *Sheffield Independent* — 4 December 1841 p.8.

8   *Illustrated London News* — 19 January 1850. p.34.

9   Robert Chambers was a local and national sporting hero. In September 1859 he beat Harry Kelly to become the Champion of the Thames, the premier event in professional sculling at the time. The month following Fanque's presentation he beat Richard A.W. Green, the Australian champion on the Thames. In 1876, the English title gained world status and earlier winners were retrospectively given the title of World Champion.

10  *Newcastle Journal* — 6 May 1863 p.2.

11  Mace had been born in Beeston, Norfolk and shared the same manager as Fanque, Harry Montague. He had already given exhibition bouts at Howes and Cushing's circus in June and July of that year. In 1862, he formed his own circus, which he subsequently sold in 1863. A full list of Mace's involvement with the circus can be found at: https://www.galatent.co.uk/jemmace/the_showman.htm accessed 22 September 2016.

12  *Sheffield Independent* — 14 September 1861 p.5. — gives his itinerary with Fanque's circus.

13  *Leeds Times* — 12 January 1861 p.4.

14  *Newcastle Daily Chronicle* — 21 May 1863 p.2.

15  *Hull and Eastern Counties Herald* — 18 March 1869 p.5.

16  *Morning Post* — 10 October 1805 p.3.

17  *Bradford Observer* — 28 June 1849 p.6.

18  *Ibid.*

19  *Ibid.*

20  *Northern Whig* — 25 March 1851 p.3.

21  *Stamford Mercury* — 27 April 1849 p.2.

22  *Preston Chronicle* — 8 December 1860 p.4.

23  *Leeds Mercury* — 7 March 1861 p.4.

24  *York Herald* — 18 January 1862 p.11. — "EXCITING SCENE.— A FEMALE 'BLONDIN' IN DANGER. Some excitement was occasioned in Preston, on Monday evening, by the announcement that a 'Female Blondin' would make a 'terrific ascent' on a tight wire to the top of the Hippodrome, in the vacant space of ground known as Chaddock's [sic] Orchard, opposite the Borough Police Office, in that town. The wire, which was about 150 feet in length, had been affixed at one end to a wooden fixture, about twelve feet high, and at the other to the square cupola, at the apex of the cirque. It was steadied by a number of guy ropes, held on either side by pegs driven in the ground. The wire was an incline, and at its maximum altitude was about 70 feet from the ground. The 'Female Blondin,' whose real name is Mrs. Potter, and who some time ago, under the professional soubriquet of Madame Salvi, travelled with Mr. Pablo Fanque's equestrian troupe, proceeded in her aerial journey, in the presence of some thousands of spectators. When she had proceeded about two-thirds of her perilous journey, it is supposed, owing to the slackness of one of the guy ropes, she lost her equilibrium, amid loud screamings and expressions of horror from the crowd below. The intrepid lady, however, with great presence of mind, in her fall, caught hold of the wire, and was thus saved from broken bones, if not a broken neck. She remained suspended in that position until the attendants at the Hippodrome, under the direction of the proprietors, Messrs. Lamb and Kitchen, could loosen the wire and lower the lady to the roof of the building. She was much shaken, but happily suffered nothing worse than an abrasion of the hands by hanging by the wire. Nothing daunted, she announced her intention to perform her dangerous feat the next evening. Mrs. Potter had a similar slip whilst performing on the tight wire at Scarborough, few months ago, and another narrow escape shortly before at Preston."

25  *Birmingham Daily Post* — 21 July 1863 p.2.

26  *Birmingham Daily Gazette* — July 1863 p.2.

27  The fete had been organised by the Order of Foresters, to raise money for the sick and funeral fund of the order in the Birmingham Midland District. — *Ibid.* 25.

28  *Ibid.* 25 — 22 July 1863 p.2.

29  *Illustrated London News* — 1 August 1863 p.111.

30  *Burnley Gazette* — 26 February 1870 p.2.

31  Walker, H. (1922) *From Sawdust to Windsor Castle*

32  *Ibid.* p.8 -10.

33  *Manchester Courier and Lancashire General Advertiser* — 25 January 1845 p.1. — "RUNAWAY. — Notice to Equestrian Managers and others, — That whereas on the 17th day of January 1845, HUGH O'DONNELL, an apprentice of Mr. Pablo Fanque, Equestrian Manager, has RUNAWAY from him; and should any of the

above parties conceal, detain, or cause to be detain, the said Hugh O'Donnell, after this advertisement appearing in the paper, proceedings will be taken against them to the full extent that the law will allow. PABLO FANQUE, Circus Royal, Oldham. Lancashire."

34 *Ibid.* — 21 February 1846 p.1. — "NOTICE TO EQUESTRIAN MANAGERS, TWO APPRENTICES having absconded from Mr. PABLO FANQUE'S CIRCUS, Bury answering to the names of MASTER PABLO FANQUE and MAST O'DONNALD, [sic] any party employing them after this notice will be liable to a prosecution. Mr.P.F. will thank any Manager to give him information should such parties apply, and to detain them until hearing from him. He will defray expenses incurred."
35 *The Era* — 3 October 1852 p.12.
36 Davin, A. *Waif Stories in Late Nineteenth-Century England.* — History Workshop Journal 52 (2001): 67-98.
37 Amy Catherine Walton published under the name Mrs. O.F. Walton.
38 Walton, O.F. *A Peep behind the Scenes* 1877 p.18. — downloadable from http://manybooks.net/titles/waltonmretexto5bescn10.html#

# 7

# The Man of Colour

*In the great brotherhood of the equestrian world there is no colour-line,*
*for although Pablo Fanque was of African extraction, he speedily made*
*his way to the top of his profession. The camaraderie of the Ring has*
*but one test, ability.*

Thomas Horne[1]

To Victorian society 'exoticism' was concerned with the perception and
description of difference. Within literature it was primarily understood
through geographical 'remoteness', while in the circus, music-hall and
fair it was provided by the performer. Many, like William Darby, adopted
what seemed strange names to their British working class audience. These
adopted names were mostly European in origin, including Fanque's,
reflecting a general cultural perception regarding 'the foreigner', that was
devoid from the colour of their skin. In all the contemporary references
to Pablo Fanque few mention his colour.

Circus was about show, flair and excitement outside the humdrum
existence of everyday life, so it was quite natural for audiences to
assume that the performers before them would have embellished names
that reflected distant places. As one historian has put it, "Like the fun-
house mirror, the circus reflected a kind of 'grotesque realism' that was
colorful, ornamental, and most of all, exaggerated but nonetheless
based on a truth about the nineteenth-century world"[2]. It is therefore
not surprising that a performer's skin colour, in newspaper and other
reports of the circus during this period, is hardly mentioned, suggesting
a lack of prejudice to later audiences.

This of course was not true when individual performers clashed with
the 'real world' outside the circus. An anecdote, related as an amusing

interlude by William Wallett in his autobiography, tells us a lot about both the covert and overt racism of the period:

> For a few days I amused myself with Pablo Fanque fishing in the Isis. Pablo was a very expert angler, and would usually catch as many fish as five or six of us within sight of him put together. This suggested a curious device. You must know that Pablo is a coloured man. One of the Oxonians, with more love for angling than skill, thought there must be something captivating in the complexion of Pablo. He resolved to try. One morning, going down to the river an hour or two earlier than usual, we were astonished to find the experimental philosophic angler with his face blacked after the most approved style of the Christy Minstrels.[3]

When presented with discrimination and prejudice Fanque did not necessarily accept it, as shown by an incident at Baslow in 1849:

> Pablo Fanque Darby, the proprietor of a travelling equestrian establishment, was charged with assaulting John Wright, of Walton, at Baslow, on the preceding day. Complainant deposed that he was servant man to Mr. Prince, and that on Friday went to Stoke, with a dray and horses for some timber. In returning he stopped at Mr. White's, the Devonshire Arms, Baslow; this was between three and four o'clock in the afternoon. Defendant's horses had been in the same stable, and when they were brought back, he (complainant) said he would take his horses (which had been put in the stable for short time by permission of Mr. White) out of the way of "that black bearded man," meaning defendant. As soon as he got to the door, defendant struck him several times.
>
> George Collis corroborated complainant's statement, as to placing the horses in the stable, and added, that when defendant returned complainant said, "Let's take the horses out of the way of that black bearded man," and was using ill language when the defendant struck him.
>
> For the defence, defendant called three young men of his *troupe*, who proved that complainant used very insulting language to their master, who did not strike until the complainant had put himself in a fighting attitude. A scuffle then ensued, in which complainant came off second best.

The Bench said they had paid great attention to the case, and the conclusion they arrived at was, that though it appeared complainant had used insulting and improper language, still they did not think that defendant was justified in striking him, and they should therefore impose a penalty of 5s and the expenses.[4]

Fanque's status in circus and cultural mythology lies in him being the first black circus proprietor. However, he was not the first black equestrian who, as Horne put it, "made his way to the top of his profession". It can be argued that Joseph Hillier, a prodigy of Andrew Ducrow, has at least equal claim to this accolade[5].

Hillier, whose nickname was, "Mungo", had been discovered by Ducrow while visiting Milan in 1820 and appeared in Ducrow's first great triumph, *Cortez, or the Conquest of Mexico*, which opened in Covent Garden on 5 November 1823. By 1827 he had his own equestrian act, based on 'Cossack' riding, in which he "rode with a most extraordinary power of retaining hold on the horse, he went full gallop, tumbling, reeling, under and over, and all about the animal, yet never coming to the ground, with really frightful clerity [sic] and cleverness"[6].

Hillier was to remain with Ducrow for over twenty years becoming the riding master at Astley's, then purchasing Ducrow's stud[7] in January 1842 following his death. He was able to finance the purchase of the stud from Ducrow's widow, having been left a legacy by the great equestrian. Like Darby, he borrowed money to make up the shortfall. Unfortunately, he was unable to keep up payments and by 1845 found himself in the insolvency court.[8]

Darby and Hillier followed in the footsteps of their heroes, Batty and Ducrow. Like so many circus performers, of which there were many, they were best placed to set up their own circuses and be part of the entertainment revolution of the period. The confidence and self-belief required to contemplate the financial outlay was enormous, but others, such as Richard Bullard, believed this new form of amusement would be a good investment and were willing to invest in their enterprises. While a few made fortunes, Darby and Hillier were far from alone in seeing their businesses fail. It took more that a 'name' to ensure success in an increasingly competitive area. It required good management and attention to financial detail. Charles W. Montague, in his autobiography, explained the necessary arrangements that needed to be made when organising a circus 'tour':

*Joseph Hillier in Ducrow's role as "The Courier of St Petersburg" at*
*Vauxhall Gardens in 1842.*

A matter of the first importance in projecting a tour is to prepare
beforehand a plentiful supply of novelties, to be produced at the
various performances, in order to serve as an additional attraction
to those who perhaps would not favour us with their patronage, did
they think that we were always grinding away, like a musical box,
at the same old themes. There must be something new and good.
Some unusually graceful or daring rider; some clever conjurer or
mirth provoking clown; some rare equine specimen, beautifully
marked and wonderfully trained — all or some of these; and
added to them, a variety of entirely new pieces for the company in
general must be secured, brought together, and worked up into an
attractive programme; proper steps being taken to let the public
know in good time what treats there are in store for them. In order
thoroughly to attain this latter point, and to make other timely
arrangements, each company sends forward an 'agent in advance'
along the identical route to be followed by the circus, and arriving

in each selected town some days, or even weeks before the date fixed for the performances. This agent's duties are multifarious and of a responsible nature; and indeed upon his shrewdness and experience not a little of the success of the tour depends. His first duty is to make prompt arrangements for thoroughly 'billing' the town — that is, displaying the large coloured pictorial and printed announcements on all the available hoardings, dead-walls, bridges, and other conspicuous places in the town and immediate neighbourhood. Then a suitable site has to be chosen on which to erect the tent with its adjuncts. Lodgings for the principals must be secured; and what is of no less importance, good stabling for the stud of valuable horses. All conveniences in fact in any way necessary for the comfort of the company are arranged beforehand, and are ready for them when they arrive. The agent in advance is to a travelling circus what scouts are to an invading army; with this difference, that he is the herald of a peaceful host which seeks no triumphs but those of Art, and strives to secure its conquests by leaving behind it in each town a strong garrison of pleasurable recollections. To complete his round of duties, the agent sends back by post to the proprietor, copies of all contracts made by him, particulars of the lodgings secured for the company, full information for the stud-groom as to which are the best stables for the more valuable horses, descriptions of the road to be traversed; and in short, places the proprietor on the same footing as though the latter had himself visited the town and made all the arrangements. It is easy to perceive that by following out this methodical system, all chance of confusion when the company arrives is entirely avoided. The agent having thus fulfilled his task, passes on to the next town, and leaves us at liberty to turn our attention to the coming guests.[9]

While Darby might be criticised by his contemporaries for financial mismanagement, he adapted to circumstances given the increased competition from his American competitors. Other British circus proprietors, such as John Frederick Ginnett, mirrored this strategy:

> ... we found upon entering the Midlands again, that our American rivals, Messrs Howes and Cushing, were playing sad havoc among

the English proprietors by the wholesale manner in which they had gone into the business. Their company had been so greatly increased in strength, that it had been divided, first into two distinct companies, then into three; and ultimately there were four American companies belonging to this single proprietary, competing keenly against us for popular support. As it is quite useless for two circuses to perform in the same town at or near the same time, this multiplication of rival establishments had the direct effect of limiting our field of operations, or rather, I should say, of compelling us to extend our operations into fresh fields and pastures new. For this reason, then, we 'took the fairs' at the various towns on our route; so that by offering special attractions, we received, in spite of the not very good state of trade in the district through which we passed, a fair share of support, and had no cause to complain of the pecuniary results.[10]

William Darby's career provides an opportunity to explore popular entertainment and how it related to the culture of the period. Entertainment developed alongside the industrial revolution, both in Britain and America, from the penny-gaff and fair culture of the theatrical booth, to the hippodrome and equestrian circus. The latter became a mainstay of popular entertainment during the 1850s, particularly following the transatlantic boom of American tented circuses. These transformed the form and nature of the circus, and although permanent buildings, as well as temporary wooden circus amphitheatres, continued well into the second half of the nineteenth century, they did begin to slowly diminish in number. By the late 1870s the business had divided into two distinct types:

It may be well to explain that there are two distinct kinds of circuses — firstly, those that perform in permanent buildings only; secondly, those that 'tent' in the spring and summer, and occupy buildings in the winter. Of the first kind there are at the time of writing (1879) five companies in the United Kingdom — namely Newsome's, Hengler's, Cooke's, Adams', and Keith's. These never perform in tents. Of the other class, there are eight recognised circuses; their proprietors being Messrs Sanger, Myers, Pinders, Batty, Powell and Clarke, F. Ginnett, G. Ginnett, and Swallow. These are the 'tenting' companies, giving their performances for the greater

*The poster which brought fame to Pablo and Mr Kite when their names were used by John Lennon.*

portion of the year in the tent which they carry about from town to town. Besides the names given, there are a few other small companies; but these are carried on by speculators only, who as a rule last but a few months, or even less than that.[11]

While circuses still revolved around equestrianism, by 1860, elephants, tigers and other exotic animals from the menageries that accompanied circuses tours, were being integrated into the ring. Such performances involved the animal cages being towed into the ring in which the 'tamers' would conduct their highly dangerous acts. The greatest exponents of this trend were George and John Sanger, who built one of the largest circuses in the second half of the nineteenth century[12]. The combination of animal acts with circus performance was perhaps an indication that audiences were no longer just content with the skill and daring of the equestrian; the introduction of exotic animals added additional danger and spice to the show. Such adaptations meant that theatres and even multi-purpose buildings, such as the Alhambra Palace, were losing their circus rings[13].

In any study of the history of popular culture[14], William Darby holds a special place. Within his lifetime both he and his circus reflected attributes of popularism — the wistful desire of a generation to recall the past, and an institution embedded in the fabric of society. In the late 20th century, his name's association with John Lennon, in the lyrics of *Being For the Benefit of Mr. Kite*, enabled another generation to identify with its call to "… challenge the world"[15]. In the first quarter of the 21st century, Fanque has become a symbol of multiculturalism, the subject of performance artistes in Britain and America[16], a Black entrepreneurial role model, and an example of how our views of the past cannot be but influenced by the cultural milieu of the present.

1   *The Era* — 26 August 1905 p.23.

2   Assael, B. (2005) *The Circus and Victorian Society.* p.154.

3   Wallett, W.F. (1884) *The Public Life of W.F. Wallett, the Queen's Jester: An Autobiography of Forty Years Professional Experience & Travels in the United Kingdom, The United States of America (including California), Canada, South America, Mexico and the West Indies etc.* p.73.

4   *Derbyshire Courier* — 8 August 1849 p.2.

5   The question of whether Hillier or Darby was the first black circus proprietor might rest with when Darby actually established his circus as a distinct entity. Wallett says this was in August 1841, whereas newspaper evidence suggests it was in January 1842, the same month that Hillier bought Ducrow's stud. It would however be accurate to say that Darby was the first African British circus proprietor, since Hillier was born in Italy.

6   *Weekly Dramatic Register* — 4 August 1827.

7   *Bell's Life in London and Sporting Chronicle* — 03 April 1842 p.2. — "The stud of the late Mr. Ducrow is now the property of Mr. Hillier, and is engaged at Sadler's Wells, and will appear shortly."

8   *Morning Advertiser* — 22 January 1845 p.4. — "He (the insolvent) has purchased of Mrs. Ducrow 17 horses and seven ponies, the stud of her late husband, for the sum of 700l., of which 270l. was paid down, which arose from a legacy from Mr. Ducrow, after deducting the legacy duty of 30l. The remainder was to be paid by instalments of 25l. a quarter, none of which however had been paid. In June 1843, when he commenced his accounts, he estimated his property at 1,200l. He has since sustained severe losses at various places, Hamburg and others mentioned in the schedule. He had some furniture, which was claimed by his mother-in-law, who had paid some rent for a house in London. It appeared that the insolvent, who is an Italian, has been in the service of Mr. Ducrow 21 years, and had been left by him the legacy mentioned. ...."

9   Montague, C.W. (1881) *Recollections of an Equestrian Manager.* p.28-30.

10  *Ibid.* p.32-33.

11  *Ibid.* p.28.

12  *Manchester Courier and Lancashire General Advertiser* — 9 March 1861 p.1. — "A GRAND WEEK OF NOVELTIES, SANGAR'S CIRCUS, THE LION KING. MR. JAMES CROOKETT, will introduce the Noble Troupe of PERFORMING LIONS. This Evening, and during the week. Go see, and believe!!!"

13  *Lloyd's Weekly Newspaper* — 30 September 1860 p.7. — "THE ALHAMBRA PALACE, after many roving years — dissolving views, scientific lectures, organs, coloured fountains, &c. the sports of the American circus, clowns, bull fights and balloons; after the ridiculous farce of Sayers and Heenan, and a fresh turn at horse racing — the Alhambra-palace, we hear will now be devoted to music." — The boxing match between Tom Sayers of England and John Heenan 17 April 1860, was regarded as the first world title match. Taking place on a field near Farnborough the police intervened as prize bare-knuckle fighting was illegal. However, both boxers were presented with silver belts at the Alhambra Palace on 30 May 1860 to mark their exploit and then conducted a tour of the country.

14  A popular culture can be identified by the following characteristics: enables ready and easy access by those that consume it; displays a cycle of local, national and global acceptance; produces commercial products that consumers use to establish links with it; and changes and evolves through time.

15  "In this way Mr. K will challenge the world" — lyrics of *Being For The Benefit Of Mr. Kite*, last line, first verse.

16  Joe Williams, a performance actor based in Leeds, has performed his one-man play, *The Fishes of Isis* in which he plays Pablo Fanque, in Britain and the United States. In the United States, Derrick Adams's performance, *Pablo Fanque's Circus Royal/SIDESHOW* pays tribute to Pablo Fanque.

# Selected Bibilography

Assael, B. (2005) *The Circus and Victorian Society.*

Booth, M. (1991) *Theatre in the Victorian Age.*

Bratton, J. and Fetherstone, A. (2006) *The Victorian Clown.*

Dickens, C. (1837) *Sketches from Boz.*

Dickens, C. (1854) *Hard Times.*

Kennedy, D. (2010) *The Oxford Companion to Theatre and Performances.*

Mayhew, H. (1861) *London Labour and London Poor, Vol III.*

McMillian, S. (2012) *Cooke's: Britain's Greatest Circus Dynasty.*

Rendell, M. (2014) *Astley's Circus: The Story of an English Hussar.*

Saxon A.H. (1968) *Enter Foot and Horse: A History of Hippodrama in England and France.*

Saxon A.H. (1978) *The Life and Art of Andrew Ducrow & the Romantic Age of the English Circus.*

Turner, J. M. (2000) *Victorian: The Performers, A Dictionary of British Circus Biography Vol II.*

Turner, J. M. (2003) *Pablo Fanque, Black Circus Proprietor* in Gretchen, H.G. (ed.) *Black Victorians, Black Victoriana.*

Turner, J.M. (1990-1991) *Pablo Fanque: "An Artiste of Colour"* in *King Pole,* 89 December 1990 and 90 January 1991.

Wallett, W. F. (1884) *The Public Life of W. F. Wallett, the Queen's Jester: An Autobiography of Forty Years Professional Experience & Travels in the United Kingdom, The United States of America (including California), Canada, South America, Mexico and the West Indies.*

# Index

Lightning Source UK Ltd.
Milton Keynes UK
UKOW05f2303280317
297770UK00001B/23/P

9 781909 796324